CONCILIUM

THEOLOGY IN THE AGE OF RENEWAL

CONCILIUM

CONCILIUM/VOL. 27

CHURCH HISTORY

PROGRESS AND DECLINE IN THE HISTORY OF CHURCH RENEWAL

edited by ROGER AUBERT

Volume 27

CONCILIUM

theology in the age of renewal

PAULIST PRESS
NEW YORK, N.Y./GLEN ROCK, N.J.

Library of Congress Catalog Card Number: 67-30136

Suggested Decimal Classification: 270

Paulist Press assumes responsibility for the accuracy of the English translations in this Volume.

PAULIST PRESS
EXECUTIVE OFFICES: 304 W. 58th Street, New York, N.Y. and 21 Harris-
town Road, Glen Rock, N.J.
Executive Publisher: John A. Carr, C.S.P.
Executive Manager: Alvin A. Illig, C.S.P.
Asst. Executive Manager: Thomas E. Comber, C.S.P.

EDITORIAL OFFICES: 304 W. 58th Street, New York, N.Y.
Editor: Kevin A. Lynch, C.S.P.
Managing Editor: Urban P. Intondi

Printed and bound in the United States of America by
The Colonial Press Inc., Clinton, Mass.

CONTENTS

PART II

BIBLIOGRAPHICAL SURVEY

PART III

DOCUMENTATION CONCILIUM
Office of the Executive Secretary
Nijmegen, Netherlands

Preface

Roger Aubert / *Louvain, Belgium*

Today's new political, social, cultural and religious situation demands that the Church find new answers to problems that are either new in themselves or at least formulated in wholly new terms. At first sight, one might think that the strictly individual character of this situation, which throughout history corresponds to one specific point in time and space, makes the past irrelevant for new solutions because one cannot apply old solutions to new, often radically different, problems. The questions are no longer the same as in the past. They have a character of their own. And yet, history can make a very valuable contribution, however trite this assertion may have become.

Of course, history does not provide us with ready-made recipes that can be applied to our situation. One of the earliest Greek philosophers had already discovered that history is something perpetually new when he said that "one can never bathe twice in the same river". But what history can teach us for the living application of Vatican Council II is the right *attitude* with which we should approach the present if we want to preserve continuity in a Church founded on tradition and yet be ready for the present demands of God. This is particularly necessary if we want to escape from the process of sclerosis that besets all institutions. Indeed, not for the first time the Church of Christ has

1

to face the task of adjusting herself to a new civilization or to a world that is undergoing a profound change.

One of the main lessons of history is that it makes us aware in a concrete fashion of the fact that from the beginning, in spite of the value of tradition, the Church has been forced to renew herself constantly, and not only at the level of the structures of the institution but—far more disconcerting for some—at the level of mentality and spirituality. At the same time history shows us that—according to whether or not Christians, both the faithful and the leaders, had the courage (or intelligence) to discover the new demands that were more or less vaguely expressed at a particular time—the Church herself progressed or declined, or even, as in the first half of the 16th century, came close to catastrophe. Therefore, it seems most important today that we should examine as objectively as possible how our ancestors in the faith reacted to situations similar to those we face today—similar in the sense of basic requirements and yet profoundly different in their historic individuality.

One could illustrate this by writing a whole history of the Church. What we have done here is not quite so ambitious. We have limited ourselves to soundings here and there. Other choices could have been made with equal justification. It is a pity, for example, that we have not been able to find room for such subjects as the transition from Jewish Christianity to Hellenistic Christianity, or the relation between Egyptian monasticism and the state of the Church under Constantine's influence, or the Gregorian reform as a spiritual phenomenon, or the reaction of the mendicant orders to the rise of the bourgeoisie in the Middle Ages, or, closer to our own age, the conflict between Catholic intellectuals and *intégristes* (hyperconservatives), or the situation of the Russian Church in a technological and atheistic world. In any event, the topics we have chosen are spread out over the period from the time when the Church was first forced to give a temporal expression to the eternal message of the Gospel (cf. Documentation) to the great confrontation—started in the 17th century and still going on today—between the unchanging principles of Christianity and the urgent demands of the "modern world". In between these two points the topics deal with the major crises of the end of the ancient world, the Renaissance and the Reformation, and with the error of the Church in attempting to impose the Western expression of Christianity on Far Eastern civilizations. We hope that these few reminders of the past may give cause for reflection to present-day pastors and theologians.

PART I
ARTICLES

Adrian Sherwin-White / *Oxford, England*

The Roman Background of Early Christianity[*]

The eastern provinces of the Roman Empire in Asia Minor, Syria and Egypt were the formative arena of the early Church. In these lands men of letters and men of business alike wrote and thought in Greek, and the civic system of the most advanced and prosperous communities was Greek. Yet a great part of the working population lived according to ancient cultures, and spoke ancient languages, which derived from the Hittite, Egyptian, Babylonian and similar civilizations of the millennium before the conquests of Alexander hellenized the East. Strange Oriental temple-domains still existed, under the control of priest-kings, with lands tilled by serfs and with companies of sacred prostitutes. In Syria, and in the plains of modern Iraq (Mesopotamia, Babylonia) beyond the Roman frontiers, Semitic languages (notably Aramaic), cults and cultures, and especially religious ideas, were common, though sometimes with a hellenized veneer in bilingual communities.

[*] This essay summarizes a vast subject in a few words. For recent general surveys of the social development of the Roman Empire, cf. J. Gagé, *Les classes sociales dans l'empire romain* (Paris, 1964); J. Balsdon (ed.), *The Romans* (New Thinkers Library) (London, 1964); A. Jones, *Decline of the Ancient World* (London, 1966); F. Millar (ed.), *Das Römische Reich und seine Nachbarn* (Fischer Weltgeschichte, Band 8) (Frankfurt a.M., 1966); A. Sherwin-White, *Roman Society and Roman Law in the New Testament* (Oxford, 1963).

7

1. *Greek Culture and Early Christianity*

The self-contained Jewish nation in Palestine, monotheistic and iconoclastic, was only the extreme instance of this Semitic ideology. But for ambitious men of all levels it was primarily a Greek world. Greek was the universal language, and Greek education was the key to advancement. From further east, beyond the Zagros mountains, yet another civilization—that of ancient Iran, with its dualist Mazdean religion and an artistic style of its own—infiltrated through Mesopotamia into the Roman Empire, bringing the cult of the warrior-divinity Mithras and the lore of the Magian astrologers.

But linguistically this culture, too, depended for its spread farther west on the dominant Greek language. Even in the villages of Syria and Egypt the Greek language made steady inroads, as is shown by the innumerable letters of humble folk from Roman Egypt. Besides, Greek was the only common tongue in the eastern regions. Once the Christian preachers began to aim at the non-Jewish world, the Greek language provided an essential means of radiating their message beyond their immediate audience. Ideas expressed in Greek could spread through a ready-made network of world communications. Still more, the internal life of the Church in her rites and formulas was bound to be molded and expressed in Greek terms.

Because the early Church was predominantly urban, Greek civilization was the decisive element in her pagan environment. Antioch, Ephesus, Iconium and Thessalonica, the scenes of St. Paul's teachings and writings and the theaters of the early martyrs, were Greek cities. They had a roughly uniform internal organization—annually elected administrators and magistrates, councils of elected or perpetual members controlling all civic activities, and assemblies of the free male population electing their local rulers. The cult of the civic gods was in the hands of these magistrates, who organized costly religious festivals which included athletic, dramatic and musical competitions, open to the professional artists of the whole Empire. These took place in the elaborate buildings of the civic "gymnasium" and theater. Humbler pleasures were provided for all citizens by the public baths, which became ever more elaborate in the prosperous peace of the Empire. Beside these blameless Greek activities there also appeared, through Roman influence, ferocious gladiatorial combats and bloody struggles between beasts in the new amphitheaters, which encouraged the uninhibited ferocity of the audience. These crude spectacles tended to oust from favor the old-fashioned comedy of manners.

In the cities, education was available in the schools of the men of letters—grammarians, rhetoricians and philosophers—who propagated the basic ideas of the Greek intellect. Though these schools consisted only of booths or halls where learned men plied their skill for private hire or a civic fee, some cities maintained libraries for public use in fine buildings, and bookshops were frequent. At times the great intellectuals of the age toured the cities and demonstrated their skills in public lectures. In this world the man of letters had great prestige. Such men, under the patronage of local kings and Roman governors, not only made fortunes but could secure high posts in the imperial administration. Equally, no doctrine, belief or social opinion could make headway in high society unless expressed in Greek thought and style. Hence came the necessity for the Greek "apologists", such as Origen, to present Greek teaching in terms that were intellectually acceptable to the educated Greek public. This meant the adoption of Greek philosophical technique and terminology for Christian theological purposes, and the rise of a mental discipline that fused the Judaeo-Christian message with the abstract concepts of Greek thought and metaphysics.

2. Roman Power

Out of the civic assemblies and the audiences of the festivals developed a new phenomenon, the city mob, much feared by the civic authorities and the Roman governors, because both were remarkably short of police forces to maintain public order.

No large units were available within the peaceful provinces, and cities maintained only the smallest detachments of civil guards at the orders of their magistrates. The repression of crime depended largely upon the initiative of private accusers in the civic or provincial courts. The city magistrate and the provincial governor were responsible mainly for sentences and their execution.

The other activities of a central government—the collection of taxes and the maintenance of many public services—were carried out by the city governments. Consequently, the individual provincial, rich or poor, was very remote from the eye of the Roman governor, and the inner life of the people largely escaped his notice. Social changes, disorders and movements, whether political, economic or intellectual, became apparent only at a late stage of their development, when it was too late for any action but acceptance or massive repression. Such movements frequently operated under the cover of social groups or clubs, organized as private religious associations. These were often officially encouraged as offering to the working masses a humble form of corporate activity that distracted them from direct intervention in the political life of the cities. Otherwise a man's prime loyalty was to his city. Even if he also happened to be a Roman citizen, the local city came first in his mind. St. Paul prided himself more on being a citizen of Tarsus, "no mean city", than on his status as a Roman.

There also came into being provincial councils, composed of representatives of the cities who met in seasonal conclaves at the various provincial capitals. These organized the cult of the emperor as a divine ruler and also acted as a political link between the provinces and Rome, sending deputations about local grievances to the emperor at Rome. Membership in these councils was an exalted provincial dignity; such were the "Asiarchs" who assisted St. Paul at Ephesus. Inevitably these institutions provided the growing Church with a pattern. The Pauline churches were civic churches, each a nucleus within an established city. Just as the city had its single magistrate, so the local church had its single "overseer" or bishop (*episcopos*). When the need for consultation between churches arose this followed the pattern of the Roman provincial councils: the churches were duly represented in their provincial assemblies and other councils by the bishops of the single cities.

3. *Social Background*

In the cities the power was effectively in the hands of the wealthy classes, whose affluence came principally from the land, the only form of permanent investment in the ancient world. Successful traders, bankers and manufacturers finally turned to land to secure the profits of their business in a durable form. The necessary articles and the luxuries of daily life, based on agricultural raw materials or on the working of metals and clay, were supplied by peasants, craftsmen and traders, through hand labor and individual enterprise, or by small workshops employing no more than a score of workers, free or servile. Particular cities became famous for a special product, such as the silver work of Ephesus, and there were certain great bazaar centers, like Damascus and Alexandria. But most cities provided work only for the necessary crafts of a limited district. Hence the economic primacy lay in land and its products. The city lived off its land, which was the private property of its citizens, and might consist of large estates worked by laborers and tenants, or of the small holdings of peasant proprietors. Most of the labor force was free rather than servile.

Slavery was endemic, but its scale is difficult to assess. Domestic slaves were numerous in the houses of the wealthy, but slavery was not a serious economic threat, it seems, to the free workers, who collaborated with slave labor in craft workshops. The treatment of domestic slaves tended to be humane: liberation and economic employment were the common reward of faithful service. The slave was as much a part of the family community as wives and children; the freed slave could enjoy as much independence as either, and was frequently more prosperous than ordinary working men. The freedmen of the emperor's household provided most of the junior personnel of the imperial bureaucracy. There were no rigid barriers between free and freed. Hence slavery presented no special difficulty to Christian morality, and could be taken for granted, as in the letter of St. Paul to Philemon.

Village life tended to model itself in miniature on the pattern of city life. But sometimes there were differences of civilization between city and village. Greek or—in the western provinces—Latin culture might prevail in cities, while the previous pattern of life and language—Celtic, Aramaic, or Anatolian—was maintained in the countryside. But the terms "town" and "city" can be misleading. Throughout the Mediterranean zones of the Roman Empire human settlement, whether agrarian or artisan, was apt to take the form of the large concentrated township, the "big village", of three or four thousand persons or more, instead of the scattered hamlets and homesteads of northern Europe. Such townships—concentrated on the hillsides through the necessities of water supply and defense, and the scarcity of rich plain land—provided a natural basis for the assimilation of the Greek or Italian style of urban civilization, but they housed the cultivators of the soil as well as the wealthy bourgeoisie.

The civic upper classes spent their surplus wealth on the voluntary adornment of their cities with fine buildings, public festivals and social endowments as much as on personal luxury and licentious living. Despite the voluptuous excesses of life at Rome itself that were alleged by the ancient satirists, the great mass of the inhabitants of the Empire lived according to the ancient conventions of family custom, and barely at subsistence level, though they could enjoy the public entertainments of the great cities within their regions. All classes, however, sought solace outside the formal civic cults of the Graeco-Roman gods, in the warm and intimate ceremonies of religious sects from Egypt, Syria and Babylonia which breached the barrier between Hellenes and non-Hellenes, Romans and provincials.

In many Greek cities Jewish immigration had established large but unofficial colonies, living "according to the Book" and organized into congregations under councils of elders. These colonies were barely tolerated by their Greek hosts, who found the Jewish way of life alien and unassimilable. There was spasmodic persecution, with city officials disrupting the Jewish organizations, although the latter were regularly protected by the Roman government. Greek intellectuals tended to approve of the austere Judaic monotheism, though not of its associated customs. Converts were made in some numbers even among Greeks, and in Egypt the Jewish population was very considerable. A society in which "Jews and Hellenes", in the language of the Acts of the Apostles, lived together was a fertile seedbed for breeding a new strain of Judaism. The Jewish colonies provided ready-made bases for Christian activity throughout the eastern regions and also at Rome itself, while the diffusion of Judaism in pagan society had prepared the way for a new monotheism free from the tiresome traditional usages of Judaism—circumcision, sabbatism, food taboos—that alienated pagan sympathies.

Upon this diversified social system was imposed the imperial organization of Rome, represented in each province by the governor and three or four high-ranking aides responsible for jurisdiction and the supervision of taxation and assisted by a bureau of clerks at the provincial capital. The Roman government affected the provincial subject through taxation and selective military service in the "auxiliary" army. Such men after twenty-five years' enlistment received Roman citizenship for themselves and their families. The local aristocrats of the cities also received Roman status in return for activity in their municipalities. This status always conferred a certain prestige and some specific advantages, such as exemption from the unrestricted jurisdiction of Roman governors, but its practical value depended upon the energy of individuals. Ambitious men could secure commissions in the Roman army and promotion thence to the middle grades of the imperial service; their sons frequently became Roman senators. Thus there arose an international hierarchy of men whose careers took them outside the bounds of civic politics into the highest cadres of the Roman State.

Mingled with the provincials who acquired Roman status,

like the father of St. Paul at Tarsus, was a considerable body of unofficial immigrants, or descendants of immigrants, of Roman status from Italy, which was the motherland of the Roman people. In addition there were a few organized colonial communities, formed originally from veterans of the Roman legions, at certain focal points in the eastern provinces, such as Beirut in Syria and Philippi and Corinth in Greece. Though not culturally predominant, these helped to integrate the various Romanizing elements. There grew up a sense of belonging to a unified system which had Rome as its center and the emperor as its head. Though difficult to define in intensity or extent, the sentiment emerges in the instructions of St. James to "honor the king". But for all persons, except the privileged few who entered the Roman administrative machine, the Roman State and its citizenship was of secondary importance to the life of the community in which they lived and worked. However, acts of misgovernment could produce different attitudes. There was a good deal of latent irritation in polished Greek society at the occasional vulgarity of Roman governors. The upper classes of Alexandria resented their subjection to Rome, and the Celts of northern Gaul as well as the inhabitants of Judaea at times fomented open rebellion. But, on the whole, oppressed provincial society seems to have distinguished between the harshness of officials and the generosity of the emperor, to whom they commonly looked for redress.

One by-product of the Roman administration was of intellectual importance. Rome generally could contribute nothing new to the life of the eastern provinces because its own culture was itself rooted in Hellenism. But Rome was original in the field of civil law and jurisprudence—the logical application of rules to the immense diversity of circumstances in problems of status, property and social behavior. Roman governors used these methods in handling the local laws of the provincial communities. Advocates and lawyers skilled in Roman law were required. Hence there arose local schools of Roman law to train provincial advocates. Roman legal science came to be known in the eastern provinces, and some of the greatest lawyers of Rome itself were of Graeco-Oriental origin. Hence the intellectual climate of the East in the 1st and 2nd centuries A.D. included not only Greek rhetoric and Greek philosophy, but Roman jurisprudence with its notions of legal contract and casuistry. This reinforced the example set by the pattern of civic and provincial government and encouraged an organization of Church life based on regulation and legal discipline. Hence, ultimately, derived the development of a complex "canon" law and the notably institutional pattern of Church life and social discipline.

A Latin-speaking region that played a great part in the development of the early Church, in counterpoise to the Greek influence, was Roman Africa (Tunisia and eastern Algeria). Here Latin literature and Roman civilization, based on the municipal system of Italy, was established early through extensive Italo-Roman colonization and the rapid assimilation of a native population of Indo-European stock, which had earlier imbibed some elements of Semitic civilization during the long period of Carthaginian domination (600-146 B.C.). Africa was a land of small cities and townships which gradually acquired the same status and usages as the cities of Italy, so that Africa became technically a Roman land. While in the East only individuals acquired Roman status, in Africa the majority of the communities became Latin and Roman in all aspects of their life. The sense of identity with Rome was immediate. Hence Tertullian in 200 A.D. can insist that the Christians of Africa were Romans, and the African Augustine later quite naturally applied the analogy of the Roman Empire to the City of God.

Jan-Maria Szymusiak, S.J. / *Warsaw, Poland*

The Barbaric Invasions and the Christian West

Fifteen years after the death of Theodosius, the city of Rome, unspoiled until then, fell under the repeated assaults of Alaric (on the night of St. Bartholomew!). At the same time the Huns reached the Elbe in the West, sacked Antioch in the East and invaded Persia. The Vandals occupied Spain before they started the conquest of the Nagreb under pressure from the Visigoths who had established themselves for the time being in central Gaul. The Burgundians settled at the sources of the Rhine and the Danube, while the Saxons seized Brittany. In a great hurry Theodosius the Young fortified Constantinople, the "New Rome", recognized under this title even by the Church at the Ecumenical Council of 381, without any protest from Pope Damasus.[1]

---

[1] I do not pretend to sum up in a few pages the eventful history of the four centuries which saw, between Theodosius and Charlemagne, the agony of a dying world. But, with many historians and psychologists, I believe that on some points this agony dragged on for over 1,000 years, while on others it still continues even after Vatican Council II. The very fact that contemporary historians of the Middle Ages are still not agreed as to the number of "Renaissances" (two, three or five), shows that certain elements of our European history, to which I limit myself here, are still alive—i.e., the time from Constantine to Charlemagne and his imitators in the Germanic "Holy Roman Empire", from Julian the Apostate to every kind of Fascist leader, from the bishop as "defender of the city" to the prelate as "interrex". All along one sees the rise of new Middle Ages, new "migrations", new "men of providence". I can

During this time the Christian communities were concerned about other things. In Africa they were debating the doctrine of grace which was threatened by Pelagius; in Egypt the passing glory of Alexandria and the assassination of the great Hypatia were subjects of concern; in the kingdom of the Sassanids they were trying to find a *modus vivendi* with the State. Was the Church worried about the barbarians? Would she fall a victim to that conservatism which she had inherited from the Roman Empire which culturally, and still more religiously, socially and artistically, had contributed nothing new during the thousand years of its existence? [2]

I

THE BEGINNING AND THE END OF ROMAN PATRIOTISM

It is hardly surprising that toward the end of the 4th century the ideas of *Romania* and *Romanitas* emerged during negotiations with the barbarians. That there is no mention of a Roman patriotism in earlier documents is not astonishing when we remember the "cellular" structure of the Empire. For the greater part of Roman history the center of Roman life was the "city", the "municipality". Consider the case of Africa, one of the most Roman provinces of the Empire. During the 5th century it consisted of a packed cluster of "City-States", each having its own curia, its temple of Rome and Augustus, and its theater for mass meetings. The Christian Church closely copied the structure of the Empire for her organization. At the summons of the Vandal king Hunneric (April, 484), 466 bishops met at Carthage (CSEL VII, pp. 117-34). They were the leaders of the Christian

only indicate a few landmarks between the first "death pangs of the classical civilization around the Mediterranean and the pregnancy of the civilization of Europe" (R. Lopez, *Naissance de l'Europe* [Paris, 1962], p. 9).

[2] Are Christians not rightly accused of being for the major part conservative-minded? See a recent investigation by M. Bergoin, J. Moreau and J. Ozouf, "Voici comment vous êtes catholique," in *Le Nouvel Observateur*, n. 106 (November 23-29, 1966).

communities in the various towns. The countryside was practically untouched, and the word "paganus" for a long time was-
used indifferently for peasant and pagan. When Byzantium became the capital under the name of Constantinople, Rome
quickly became a municipality like all the others. The emperors
of the West stayed mainly in Milan or Trier. But for over a
century they were mainly peripatetic sovereigns, and whenever
an emperor made his entry into a municipality, the occasion was
celebrated as his *dies natalis* (birthday) in Latin, or his *epiphany*
in Greek.

Yet, at the time of St. Ambrose, Bishop of Milan, who was one
of the first to appeal to Roman patriotism in order to explain
the duty of Christians toward the State (e.g., *De Officiis* II, 15,
71; 28, 136; III, 3, 23; 13, 84: P.L. 16, 123; 140A; 151C;
169C), the word "Romania" occurs in Book XVI of the *Res
Gestae* of Ammianus Marcellinus (Ch. XI, 7) to designate the
territory covered by the Empire.[3]

One has but to read the laments of St. Jerome in his letters
(e.g., *Ep. ad Heliod.* 60, 16: P.L. 22, 600; *Ep. ad Principiam
virg.* 127, 12: P.L. 22, 1094), and his prefaces to Books I, III
and VII of his commentary on Ezechiel (P.L. 25, 15; 25, 75D;
25, 199A) to see that Roman patriotism at that time was not an
empty word.[4]

For the citizens of the Empire the word "barbarian" no
longer meant the same as in classical Greek. Originally it referred to those who did not speak Greek (in other words, those
who "talk gibberish" (*bar-agouinent*), just as the Slavs use *slovo*
for those who speak the language, and *niemcy* (dumb) for those

---

[3] At least in the *Ms. Vatic. 1863* (*"contra utilitatem Romaniae fe-
cisse"*). The text seems to date from 390. But this *Romania* also appears
in a text which may be some months, if not years, older, the *Dissertatio
Maximi contra Ambrosium* (P.L., Suppl. I, 706). The historians commonly attribute the origin of the term to Orosius, whose work *Historiarum adv. Paganos libri VII* appeared a quarter of a century later
(III, 20 and VII, 43: P.L. 31, 840A, 1172B).

[4] In the same vein, see Ep. 99 of St. Augustine, *Ad Italicam* (P.L. 37,
365); Sermon 81 (P.L. 38, 506), etc. See also the Greek inscription
quoted by R. Lopez (*op. cit.*, p. 24): "Lord Christ, protect Romania."

that do not). But from the time of Alexander's conquests and the popular harangues of the cynical philosophers, influenced by the Stoa, the meaning of "barbarism" became much more relative. With the Roman conquest and the extension of citizenship by Caracalla, only those people who lived beyond the frontier were called "barbarian". For the Christians of the 4th century, whatever was not Roman was barbarian; only those were "cultured" who had accepted Christianity or who lived in its ambiance. And so what was not Christian was barbarian.[5] It then becomes understandable that all those who belonged to *Romania* felt a common sense of danger in the presence of successive waves of invasion by people who were instinctively looked on as savages.

And yet these expressions of Roman patriotism cannot be considered nationalistic. For example, Salvian of Marseilles does not hesitate to praise the virtues of those barbarians whom the "right-minded" looked on as the tools of Satan; nevertheless, one has but to read Isidore of Seville (end of the 6th century) to see that the old particularism had become dominant again, at least in the provinces.[6] It is at least certain that, as the Empire

[5] Even in the 9th or 10th century the Slavic tribes that had been organized into a Christian State under the Polish Duke Boleslaw were contrasted with the "gentes barbarorum", in *Chronica Polonorum* (MGH Scriptores IX, 1, c. 11; cf. *Mon. Hist. Pol. II* [Cracow, 1952], c. 11). The evolution of the meaning of the word pursued its course. In the Middle Ages it lost its sharp edge; the biblical term "nationes" or "gentes" was used for non-Christian peoples. The humanists of the 16th century used it derisively for the German nation whose ancestors had, according to them, killed the *romanitas*. As for the peoples more recently evangelized in the Far East, the missionaries, particularly the Jesuits, described them rather as "idolaters", never as "barbarians".

[6] Apparently Isidore did not use the expression "We barbarians" so often attributed to him. But he is full of praise for the barbarian kings Sisebut and Suintilla who had become Catholic and delivered Spain from the "Romans" (cf. *Hist. de regibus Gothorum* . . . 62-67: P.L. 83, 1074-5). But it must be pointed out that those "Romans" who were "subjected to the yoke of the Goths" after they had oppressed Spain were Byzantine troops. One may gauge the gap between the Latin and Greek cultures by the fact that the archdeacon Gregory, who died as pope in 604, never dreamed of learning Greek during the six years he spent in Constantinople. Two hundred years earlier the emperor of the East, Valens, also did not know the language of his subjects when he died in the disaster of Andrinopolis; however, at that time generals were not required to have a university degree.

disintegrated under the blows of the barbarians, the cities returned to their original position of "City-States", cut off from
the central government and often reduced to an urban center,
surrounded by walls, protected by a garrison, and more or less
independent of an emperor who was too far away or powerless.
The people of the countryside were left to their sad fate unless
they found one of those large landowners whose "villa", instead
of being turned into a fortress, frequently became a kind of head-
quarters for the barbarians where victors and vanquished lived
together more or less on the basis of the imperial law of "hos-
pitality" due to "federated troops" (398; *Cod. Theod.* VIII, 8, 5)
or on that of the "customs" of the invaders.

II

THE BISHOP AS "DEFENSOR CIVITATIS" (DEFENDER OF THE CITY)

At this time we are still far from a European "Christendom".
With no central government and the breakdown of the local institutions, only the administration of the Church, based on that
of the Empire, survived. Soon the whole of the West was taken
away from the Empire. But the towns with their protective walls
organized themselves around the one person who was still relatively independent of the barbarians, the bishop. Dedicated to
his people, often elected because of his organizing ability or even
his warlike qualities, he became the "defender of the city", sometimes humiliated but usually respected by the invader who either
felt some superstitious fear or was impressed by his personality,
without any considerations of a spiritual kind.

One could write a whole chapter on how the notion of the
papacy developed in those troubled days. During the previous
century the very fact that the emperor was no longer there gave
the Bishop of Rome more freedom of action than the bishop of
the capital, whether the capital was Nicomedia, Trier or Milan.[7]

[7] To be fair, one ought to make some qualifications in the case of
Milan because of the personality of Ambrose. But even he could not
do anything when, like St. Martin of Tours, he tried to intervene in

Although cooperation between Church and State had begun on the principle of separation of powers, the Christian emperors very soon found themselves involved in theological quarrels which degenerated into prestige conflicts between metropolitan cities.[8] In many cases the Church leaders had not hesitated to effect a compromise with the State authorities.[9]

This situation also developed in the barbarian States of the West, with the exception of Africa which was subjected to a ruthless persecution, described in sufficient detail by Victor, Bishop of Vita. Yet in Theodoric's "kingdom of Italy" Pope Gelasius I took it upon himself to propound the theory of the two powers in a letter to Emperor Anastasius, just as he had reminded his predecessor of the words of St. Ambrose: "The emperor is a son of the Church, not a superintendent (*episcopus*) of the Church." Here he said: "This world is governed by two principles: the sacred authority of the pontiffs and the royal power." [10] Pope John I died in prison for not having succeeded in his mission to the Emperor of Byzantium with which Theodoric had charged him. Justinian unhesitatingly took Church matters again into his own hands. The Lombard invasion freed the Bishop of Rome again from the hold the emperor had over him and allowed him to consolidate his patriarchal supremacy over the West. Gregory the Great who resided in Rome—nominally Byzantine territory but in reality a kind of no-man's-land between opposing forces —found that he had to act as a temporal sovereign in spite of himself. He mediated between the Byzantines and the Lombards, rallied under his authority those provinces that were deprived of

---

Trier in favor of Priscillian and his disciples who were condemned to death by the emperor (and usurper) Maximus.

[8] See G. Bardy, "Alexandrie, Antioche, Constantinople, 325-451," in *L'Eglise et les Eglises* I (Coll. Irenikon) (Chevetogne, 1954), pp. 183-207; H. Rahner, "Vom Ersten zum Dritten Rom," in *Abendland* (Freiburg im Br., 1966), pp. 253-69.

[9] Is it necessary to recall the toadyism of Ennodius of Pavia who makes Theodoric a new "Pontifex Maximus" (P.L. 69, 181C)?

[10] The first letter dates from the pontificate of Felix II, to whom Gelasius was secretary; the second dates from 494 (A. Thiel, *Epistolae Romanorum Pontificum* [Braunsberg, 1868], pp. 293, 349-54).

an effective government, and finally sent a group of missionaries to the Angles by which he brought under Roman obedience a whole barbarian nation, which until then had been neglected from the spiritual point of view. Through its own internal strength this mission spilled over on the neighboring continent northward, and one may reasonably assert that the Anglo-Saxon churches in the 6th century, the Frisian ones in the 7th century (to which the Lombard converts should be added), and the German ones in the 8th century strengthened the ties with the pope—thanks to their own direct link with Rome—in the older churches (Milan, Aquileia, Ravenna, Lyons) that had been in large measure disorganized. Some historians see in this process a first step toward the European community of the Middle Ages.[11]

On their part, the bishops of Gaul and Spain worked diligently to unify their regions. Finally the monastic communities took up the functions of the urban centers of old. It was not mere accident that St. Benedict chose John the Baptist, the precursor of the Lord, and Martin of Tours, the great missionary of Gaul, as protectors of his first abbey of Monte Cassino. If Benedict chose to remain a layman, it is because—in spite of the preponderant part played by bishops of the caliber of Cesarius of Arles and Gregory of Tours in Gaul, and Martin of Braga and Leander in Spain—the People of God had not yet completely lost the sense of its place in the Church. Nevertheless, we have to wait until the 20th century before a solemn document of the Church, crowning the efforts of a whole generation, recalls that "the laity likewise share in the priestly, prophetic and royal office of Christ and therefore have their own share in the mission of the whole People of God in the Church and in the world" (*Decree on the Apostolate of the Laity*, n. 2). We do not, of course,

---

[11] For the East, people usually mention the apostolate of Ulphilas among the Goths whom he converted from Arianism. We should not overlook the work of John Chrysostom who encouraged the liturgical life of the Goths who lived in the capital and gave them preachers who could speak their own language as well as liturgical texts in the vernacular. The same holds for Nicetas of Remesiana and at least Severinus on the banks of the Danube, who are still less known (cf. CSEL IX, 2).

regard the laity of today on the same level as the barbarians of the 6th-8th centuries. It is, however, a fact that there are still a number of bishops, no doubt full of zeal for their flocks, who regard the laity as second-rate members of the Church. They seem to act as if they have forgotten that the mass of God's people is constituted by the laity, and that they themselves have to serve as well as to command in the Church (*Constitution on the Church*, nn. 24, 32).

It is true that a considerable number of bishops of that time went through a period of apprenticeship in clericalism—if it is necessary to go through such an apprenticeship when one has allowed purely political or mercenary tendencies to grow within oneself. The fact is that the people gradually lost the sense of their responsibilities in the Church while the clergy did nothing to counteract this regression in their frequent confusion of the spiritual domain with the various activities of the purely temporal. Jacques Le Goff rightly made the ironical observation that "the decadence of the Merovingian monarchy and that of the clergy go together" because "in the end, bishops and kings who wanted to prop each other up, neutralized and finally paralyzed each other".[12] That was one of the results of the barbarian occupation of the West.

However, there were two consequences of the invasions that can hardly be overestimated. The first is that many a Christian community was forced to lead a life more worthy of the children of God. The second is that they saved the Western Church from slipping into nationalistic individualism and the evil of auto-cephalous divisions.

[12] J. Le Goff, *La civilisation de l'Occident médiéval* (Paris, 1964), pp. 62-63. Although remarkable and no doubt excellent for the Middle Ages, this work does not show a thorough knowledge of the sources for the period of transition, of which I have presented some features. Moreover, the theological assertions, which a historian cannot avoid in a work about a whole culture, are too hasty and not borne out by the texts. Other statements, such as those about the art of rhetoric (*op. cit.*, p. 151), become rather mystifying when the author seems to ignore that the Christian homily, particularly among the Fathers of the Church in the 4th century, was more than a mere exercise in style without character or precise aim.

st maintained for a long time the basilica of the time of
1stantine (e.g., St. Mary of the Source at Constantinople)
l the rotunda shape, like the plan of Agrippa's Pantheon, or
octagonal shape of the baptistry of the Lateran. An evolu-
1 rather than a break shows in the two great Byzantine inno-
ons, the domed basilica which combines the two first forms
ttioned above (of which the new church of Santa Sophia,
iilt by Justinian, is the masterpiece), and the cruciform shape
linary cross or Greek cross) which never lost its popularity.

age of Charlemagne created nothing new except for the
that at this time the altar began to be more separated from
faithful. Even the pointed arch had its prototype in the
istry of Nocera in Italy (5th century) if it is genuine. As to
cosmic symbolism, so beloved by certain mystical-minded
mentators on a too heavenly-minded liturgy, it would appear
e derived from the Roman paganism of the cupola of the
heon and the vaults of the Mithraeum.

ut this continuity with antiquity in the monumental arts is
nificant compared with the efforts to maintain the intellectual
inuity. Rhetoric reached its peak in the 4th century both in
ine literature, with Libanios and Julian, and in the oratory
homilies of the great Cappadocians and John Chrysostom in
:ast, who set the tone for the Byzantine schools right up to
atastrophe of 1453, and of St. Augustine and his followers
e West. Dialectics, introduced into theology at the time of
.rian conflict, and with some advantage in that field, became
najor influence in the 12th century, flourished in the rich
.asticism of the 13th, degenerated into nominalism and
:d again in the Neo-Scholasticism of the 19th century. On
point, as on so many others, it needed the confrontation of
ithers of Vatican Council II with the schemas prepared in
too formal and traditionalist way by the curia before we

---

people had adopted the "short" dress of the barbarians, the clergy
nstructed to wear the traditional "long" dress of Rome. Here, too,
centuries were needed before in certain Christian regions the
began to dress like an ordinary man. And this evolution is not yet
d; in most places it has not even started.

III

THE CONTINUITY AND DISCONTINUITY OF THE

The "donation of Pepin" of 754 was partly
a factual situation and partly the setting up of
torate in the middle of territories occupied
Without going into the details, one has to s
the Papal States was the first radical break
inaugurated a medieval situation which or
Lateran Agreement of 1929. Whether consc
and Charlemagne thereby introduced a ter
the Church which, in the course of the cer
more than once to be one of the most powe
spiritual *élan* of a free Church that was
souls.

As to the political ideal of a "Roman
fascinated the Germans from the 6th cent
with many fluctuations and varieties, up
20th century. One can consider this an asp
of the ancient world.

On the other hand, monasticism, wha
who are too keen on finding syncretism
was a purely Christian phenomenon—at
forms which prevailed after the early stag
any case)—of an anarchical explosion o

A more detailed study would also ha
tinuity in the art of building, both in the
of old material and in the persistence
spite of an influence from the steppes in
goldsmith's craft and dress.[18] In archi

---

[18] This would be the place for a history
the time that Eustathius, the pioneer of mon
humiliated by his own father at the Synod
cause he wanted to wear something differer
time when the pope bitterly reproached St.
tury later, for letting the monks of Lerins
diocese wear a costume that was different f
bers of the Christian community. On the

could rediscover the living source of a tradition that had dried up prematurely because it had been severed from Scripture.

This many-sided development had its rudiments in the works of the scholars of the barbarian epoch and of the Carolingian Renaissance; they never concealed their desire to save the ancient heritage. The enthusiasm of the Christians of Rome at the end of the 3rd century, who had a liturgy in their own popular idiom, was no less than that of today's Christians who can now worship publicly in the vernacular; unity is not the same as uniformity. Those responsible for the thousand years of Latin in the prayers of the Church and her teaching of theology were the great pioneers of the time of Theodoric: Boetius, the master logician of the Middle Ages, and Cassiodorus, whose official correspondence, bound together, served as the diplomatic textbook for all the chanceries of Europe until the end of the 18th century and even beyond. Throughout the "dark ages" the great educators were, apart from the two just mentioned, Pope Gregory the Great in the field of morality, Isidore of Seville with his encyclopedic compilations, Alcuin the reformer, John Scotus Erigena (particularly through his translation of Pseudo-Dionysius, practically abandoned by the Greek-speaking world since the 7th century) and all those who continued along the lines of St. Augustine with more or less happy results.

These too sketchy notes give only a very feeble notion of the explosion of vitality and the great upheavals that followed the occupation of Rome by the hordes of Alaric up to the Carolingian settlement. The Church of the 20th century stands, without any doubt, at a decisive turn on the ill-defined road of her earthly pilgrimage. As long as she is to any extent interested in the world in which God makes her live, she can never cease adjusting herself to the "barbarians", however loud the protests of those who think that "she is going too fast". It is indeed heartrending when one sees far too often that instead of taking root in the living present in order to unfold the branches of the tree of life to all the horizons of humanity, she tends to get bogged down in a dying past, the values of which cannot be denied but the disintegration of which is inevitable. She took the right turn at the time of Constantine, but Vatican Council II has shown only too clearly that it is high time for her to leave it behind if she does not want again to be found, at least in certain fields, to be several generations behind a fully developed world, of which she has to be the leaven of constant renewal. The historian of the "dark ages" is no doubt aware of her many weaknesses but he cannot help believing in the eternal youth of a Church which is constantly reborn.

Anton Weiler/*Nijmegen, Netherlands*

The Christian Humanism
of the Renaissance
and Scholasticism

In the present ecumenical atmosphere we no longer object to a serious study of the relations between Catholicism and the Reformation. The genuine Christian value of the great Reformers' efforts to renew the Church on the lines of a new understanding of Scripture is no longer questioned. On the contrary, some are convinced that the demands of the Reformation must be realized within the old Catholic Church if we want to bring about Christian unity effectively.

However, in the discussion of the kind of thought that is linked, in one way or another, with the Renaissance (1300-1600), our attitude is still hesitant. This attitude still identifies that humanism with paganism and atheism with the result that the so-called Christian humanism is still looked on as a somewhat feeble and ineffectual compromise. There is still a great fear that the dialogue with the humanism of that era as with that of the present will result in a "naturalization" of religion, the vanishing of the exclusively revealed character of Christianity, and consequently an evaporation of dogma and a weakening of the magisterium; Christianity as a doctrine of salvation would yield to a universal and personalist ethics.

Therefore, while we now accept Protestantism as a believing and Christian partner with whom we can enter upon a dialogue, we avoid the dialogue with humanism which is considered to be a-Christian and unbelieving, and hence suspect. We would do well to realize that before the call to reform had found expression in a new denomination, humanism had already been in existence for one century and a half, had definite religious and ethical views, had asked for a hearing and was given that hearing within the Catholic Church of Western Europe. This humanism has more long-standing claims to a dialogue, but they were overruled by those made for Protestantism. However, we cannot reasonably bypass this humanist contribution to religion and morality.

I

ORIGIN AND NATURE OF THE HUMANISM OF THE RENAISSANCE

Modern history has given increasing attention to the religious aspects of humanism. The futile debate about the pagan or Christian character of this period (1300-1600) has died down because scholars have abandoned the attempt to compress all the dimensions of the Renaissance mind within one all-encompassing formula. The period is now allowed to speak for itself, with all its complexity. Thus the situation has become clearer than it was at the time of the fierce controversy which followed the publication of Jacob Burckhardt's great work when authors like H. Thode, K. Burdach, L. von Pastor, X. Wernle, E. Walse and G. Toffanin discussed the matter of how to christen the whole of the Renaissance.[1]

First of all, the terminology has been clarified. The studies of P. O. Kristeller[2] and A. Campana,[3] following the lines indicated

[1] Cf. W. Ferguson, *The Renaissance in Historical Thought. Five Centuries of Interpretation* (Boston, 1948); T. Helton, *Renaissance: A Reconsideration of the Theories and Interpretations* (Madison, 1962); H. Schulte Nordholt, *Het beeld der Renaissance. Een historiografische studie* (Amsterdam, 1948).

[2] "Humanism and Scholasticism in the Italian Renaissance," in *Byzantion* 17 (1944), pp. 346-74.

[3] "The Origin of the Word 'Humanist,'" in *Journal of the Warburg and Courtauld Institutes* 9 (1946), pp. 60-73.

by J. Huizinga,[4] have established that the term "humanist" as used in the 15th century simply referred to the professor, student or amateur of the *studia humaniora,* which comprised grammar (Latin language and literature), poetry, rhetoric, history and, finally, moral philosophy and Greek. The broader philosophy of life was only a secondary element because, indeed, the humanist meant to improve and equip the human condition by means of this study of the humanities. The new interest in truly classical speech as the best means for cultural communication brought with it the passionate study of Latin—and later also Greek— antiquity, leading to a new ethical approach to human living.

Secondly, it is now recognized more than before that humanism was not a mere playing about with the ancient culture of poets and great minds in a way which did not substantially affect their own attitudes;[5] rather, this interest in antiquity was inspired by a new awareness of man, and this demanded new norms (based on antiquity) because the old ones were no longer thought valid in a changed society. The position is therefore not that the new study of antiquity created a new man but rather that the new man turned to antiquity for new standards. The rise of a free middle class—a process which had already started in Italy and Flanders in the 11th century and had shaped an urban civilization where people could escape from feudal social coercion ("the air of the town is a free air")—not only disrupted the social structure but also its ideological justification.[6]

The structures of feudal society were underpinned by an ideology that ran in strict hierarchical patterns.[7] The dominant

[4] "Het probleem der Renaissance," in *De Gids* 84 (1920); also in *Verzamelde Werken* IV (Haarlem, 1949), pp. 231-75.

[5] Cf., for example, an early (1914) essay by E. Walser, "Christentum und Antike in der Auffassung der italienischen Frührenaissance," in *Studien zur Geistesgeschichte der Renaissance* (Basle, 1932), pp. 48-63.

[6] A. Martin, *Soziologie der Renaissance* (Stuttgart, 1932); L. Martines, *The Social World of the Florentine Humanists, 1390-1460* (Princeton, 1963).

[7] Cf., for example, J. Wright, *The Order of the Universe in the Theology of St. Thomas Aquinas* (Rome, 1957); R. Roques, *L'univers dionysien. Structure hiérarchique du monde selon le Pseudo-Denys* (Paris, 1954).

elements here derived from the Stoa and Neo-Platonism. But after Augustine and Pseudo-Dionysius had worked them over, it took on the appearance of an eminently Christian doctrine: the hierarchical order, created by God in the *cosmos* (the ordered world), is realized and guaranteed on this earth by the basic institutions of empire and Church, which are, in turn, hierarchically structured. In a feudalism which was predominantly agrarian, every man had the place that God and the order of the world had assigned to him. Holiness consisted in conforming to this order and was achieved by obeying the orders that came from the top, through which orders God's will was translated for man in practical terms; all he had to be concerned with was to know his place.

But with the 11th-century rise of commerce, the Crusades and the discoveries that followed in their wake, this same man rediscovered himself. He began to see that, with others, he was capable of acquiring such wealth as would enable him to replace this dependence of the individual by a communal, thoroughly organized society to which the hierarchical powers had to yield. A new middle-class elite was born, bearer of a new power— namely, that of economics. In this opening up of new vistas "man discovered himself and his world". This formula of Burckhardt's, for a long time rejected as a too exclusive and one-sided interpretation, is again more and more accepted by historians, in spite of the deeper understanding of the medieval roots of Renaissance society. The new material provided by that intellectual aspect of history which Burckhardt himself neglected seems to argue the truth of his vision. Nicola Abbagnano recently defined the basic features of the humanism of the Italian Renaissance wholly in the light of this "newness": a new art, a new outlook on the world, a new conception of the role of science, a new approach to history and politics, a new vision of man as a communal being and as an individual, a new view of the function of religion. And so there was a real break with the medieval world, which, from the second half of the 14th century on, was consciously expressed by the contemporary elite as the enthusiastically accepted rebirth of the spirit of man, inspired by classical antiquity. Abbagnano characterizes this spirit as "a spirit of freedom by which man vindicates his rational autonomy, recognizes himself as deeply implanted in nature and in history, and is determined to make these his dominion".[8]

The mentality of the classics found a new and nourishing soil in the growing emancipation of urban culture within the walls of the human communities of north and central Italy, where the profit motive inaugurated a free economy, the money economy replaced the land economy, the civic corporations became the dominant center of civil and commercial life instead of the feudal aristocracy, and leadership was taken over by gifted individuals. This consciously expanding atmosphere gave birth to that social dynamism which replaced the ideology of a rigid, hierarchical and pre-determined natural order, tied up with the eternal magic of birth and death, by the mobile ideology of a creation that is eternally subject to the process of "becoming".[9] Thus, humanism in the broad sense can be seen as the belated philosophical expression of what had already been for centuries the practical reality, economically and politically, particularly in the Italian cities[10] where the typical features of the Middle Ages were far less fixed than in France. The full consequences of this sociological and ideological restructuring of society became obvious only centuries later.

II

THE NEW FREEDOM AND ITS RELATION TO CLASSICAL ANTIQUITY

The topics about which these Italian aristocrats, rich merchants, bankers, officers and secretaries of the papal court, the

[8] "Italian Renaissance Humanism," in *Cahiers d'Histoire mondiale* 7 (1962), p. 267, an excellent summary of the main themes of Italian humanism.

[9] L. Philippart, "Essai sur le mot et la notion d'humanisme," in *Revue de Synthèse* 9 (1935), pp. 102-16, 203-13.

[10] Abbagnano, *op. cit.* (see n. 8), p. 270.

princely court or the municipal corporation conversed were always centered on the newly discovered freedom.[11] They were no longer interested in the traditional order but looked on themselves as rational and free human beings, quite capable of planning and realizing their own destiny in nature and history. To be human did not mean for them to be exiles from an ideal world in a material one, from paradise in a communal existence dominated by original sin and where the only way to salvation lay in a flight from the world and asceticism. That man belongs to this earth and this world was fully accepted, and this was seen as man's own domain, subject to his own creative power. They looked with new eyes on the body, the senses, pleasure, sex, just as they looked on civic obligations toward the political community in a new light. The independently-taken initiative carried the process of man's self-realization in freedom much further than before when it was hampered by the individual and social limits laid down by the Church and a feudal society.

This new attitude toward man's existence found nourishment in classical literature where the inspiration of nature was not yet incapsulated in Christian ethics and where the wings of human dynamism had not yet been clipped by monastic religiosity. Contemporary medieval-Christian attitudes still regarded contemplative life as superior to active life. The Scholastic philosopher was still more interested in logic, physics and metaphysics, in legalism and the right order of things, than in a moral philosophy that would equip man for his existence. The theologian had built up his image of God and the world according to static and hierarchical visions that corresponded closely to feudal custom, and the inner practice of religion seemed to dissolve in asceticism. The new urban society *could* not take its cue from the Christian attitude as it had prevailed until then because this attitude had never been confronted with this new self-determining man and it lacked the intellectual framework for this situation.

---

[11] M. Seidlmayer, "Petrarca, das Urbild des Humanisten," in *Wege und Wandlungen des Humanismus. Studien zu seinen politischen, ethischen, religiösen Problemen* (Göttingen, 1965), pp. 125-73.

There was a sudden and new interest in classical literature, and its free, uninhibited thinking only then became an inspiration for this new and active man.

Antiquity appeared to them as a golden age, the historical moment when man freely determined his own shape, one not denaturalized by inhibiting systems. There was a desire to recapture this age; the perfect expression of man's own image had to be brought to life again in a new golden age which dawned upon man after the dark age of monkish ignorance and aristocratic and clerical domination. Thus the Middle Ages and the Renaissance came to be distinguished as different historical periods on the basis of the newly-awakened sense of historical development. The new man no longer saw himself as a timeless fixture in the all-determining order of Church and world; on the contrary, there was room for decline and decadence, as well as for revival and renaissance. The process of history, now for the first time thought about as of value for itself, was still seen as a circular process, a return to the beginning, but man himself was now seen as its active principle, and it was man who hauled the golden age from the past and brought it again to life.[12]

III

THE CONFLICT WITH THE FEUDAL CHURCH AND SCHOLASTICISM

It is obvious that the changing outlook of a changing society was bound to have repercussions on man's view of God and religion. There, too, the process was at work with the idea of freedom and the historicity of man's existence. In the Church and Christendom, people began to contrast the historical decline of the past with the ideal beginning of the present. Particularly

[12] Still basic are: K. Burdach, "Sinn und Ursprung der Worte Renaissance und Reformation. Ein Kapitel zur deutschen Wortgeschichte," in *Renaissance, Reformation und Humanismus* (Berlin, ²1926); K. Borinski, *Die Weltwiedergeburtsidee in der neueren Zeiten* (Klasse, 1919), pp. 1-130.

striking was the way in which the Church and the concrete aspect of her institutions were subjected to a fierce criticism which took the idealized community of the early Church as the norm for its judgment.[13] The humanists were prominent in exposing the critical situation of the Church, brought about by the lust for power in the curia and the bribery and the moral corruption of its leaders. But, as M. Seidlmayer has pointed out, this criticism was not the preserve of the humanists; throughout the Middle Ages heretics and reformers called for a return to the "apostolic life" of the early Church. "Such unhampered criticism shows the broad-mindedness which medieval man still possessed in spite of everything and which only fell a victim to the nervous discipline of the ecclesiastical system in the new age." [14]

When all is said and done, this outward historical connection of the Church with the secular power and all that this implied was not what concerned the humanist most. The tension between him and the Church lay rather in the basic questions about what form of Christian life was the right one for an increasingly independent humanity that was no longer satisfied with the monastic, hierarchical and authoritarian ethics of conventional Christendom. People asked for a new and more personalist approach. Protest against the traditional habit of reducing Christian life to a monklike existence was vocal, and attempts were made to draw from a Gospel purified by literary criticism, and with the help of elements of classical morality, some basic principles that might lead to a positive and new lay theology. The new Christian understanding the layman had of himself was no longer interested in the traditional system of Scholasticism, whether in philosophy or theology. Definitions of faith and proofs for God's existence did not concern him. Aristotelian speculation only obscured one's sight of the simple revelation and should therefore not be heard where the inspiration of a Christian life was concerned.

From the days of Francesco Petrarca (Petrarch), the father

[13] P. Mestwerdt, *Die Anfänge des Erasmus. Humanismus und Devotio Moderna* (Leipzig, 1917), p. 31.

[14] M. Seidlmayer, "Religiös-ethische Probleme des italienischen Humanismus," in *Wege und Wandlungen* (see n. 11), p. 275.

and prototype of humanism,[15] one can follow this opposition to the Scholastics, the academic theologians and philosophers of the universities. For Petrarca these were the Italian disciples of Averroes (Ibn Roeschd, d. 1198), the Arab commentator of Aristotle who, in an attempt to purge the Aristotelian tradition from Neo-Platonist elements, had concluded that, insofar as thought was concerned, natural reason could not be reconciled with revelation. Philosophically speaking, there could be no question of creation or of personal immortality, and no genuine Aristotelian would allow any theological faculty to dictate to him that he had to maintain the contrary, even in philosophy. And so the Italian universities—which had no completely equipped theological faculty but rather provided training for medicine or law—taught a philosophy which freely pursued the path of an a-Christian naturalistic Aristotelianism that E. Gilson has described as "the learned expression of fundamental unbelief",[16] barely masked by outward loyalty to the Church. Others have given a more innocent interpretation of this ecclesiastically condemned Averroism, pointing out that in the Italian universities this was simply an Aristotelianism pursued by medical men and not by theologians.[17]

The point is here that this academic philosophy nowhere touched man's concrete existence and therefore provided no inspiration for man's life as he lived it from day to day, apart from the fact that it was condemned by the Church. The early humanists were not in the least interested in questioning the truth of the Christian faith for the sake of philosophy. Christ was far more important to Petrarca than Aristotle, even though the philosophers despised him for his ignorance and for only seeing cultural value in beautiful language.

[15] See n. 11.

[16] E. Gilson, *La philosophie au Moyen Age* (Paris, ²1952), p. 691: "The Averroism of Jean de Jandun is therefore probably a learned expression of religious unbelief and one could consider him an ancestor of the libertines."

[17] P. Kristeller, *Die italienischen Universitäten der Renaissance* (Krefeld, 1964); B. Nardi, *Saggi sul Aristotelismo padovano dal secolo XIV al XVI* (Florence, 1958).

In France and Germany the academic philosophy of the universities was considered equally irrelevant. Since the short-lived marriage of the Christian faith with Aristotelianism, brought about by Albert the Great and St. Thomas, had been dissolved by the condemnation of a great number of Aristotelian propositions in 1277, a rift appeared [18] which made it difficult for the magisterium to maintain that spiritual unity of thought and belief as the expression of the basic cosmic harmony of which God as creator and revealer was the magnetic center. Some went back to the traditional patterns of thought of Augustinianism, while others tried to develop or adapt St. Thomas's synthesis in spite of the historical situation. But a very important group abandoned in principle all efforts at reconciliation that doubted the value of reason in the field of metaphysics and natural theology. Whole new fields lay open where there was no chance of running into conflict with theology; speculative logic studied the manifold functions of the terms in a grammatical sentence in new categories without bothering about the ontological foundation of the human judgment which made use of these terms. This was accompanied by more interest in natural philosophy where new insights paved the way toward natural sciences which developed on the lines of experiment and mathematics.

But even this development offered no prospects for that new urban type of man, particularly in that important center, Florence. By the end of the 14th century they were mainly interested in the State and in maintaining a republican freedom against the threat of the Visconti tyranny which spread from Milan over the whole of northern and central Italy. And here we reach an important moment in this history, a moment that was decisive for the future development of humanism. In these days of danger the Florentines managed to turn this early humanism—which was inspired by the classics and indulged in aesthetics, but which was politically and socially still uncommitted—into a new concept

[18] Apart from the usual textbooks, see the fine synthesis of D. Knowles, *The Evolution of Medieval Thought*, especially the section "The Breakdown of the Medieval Synthesis" (London, 1962), pp. 291-336.

of citizenship, based on patriotism, an active and political service of the community and the defense of freedom.[19] Citizenship, the family, the priority of active political life above that of the solitary contemplative scholar, the substitution of the ideal of a free and republican Rome for that of imperial Rome, the futility of philological disputations without any social relevance—all these topics flowed from the new "civic" orientation of Florentine humanism after 1400. However, one should remember that this "civic" or "civilian" orientation refers to the top layer of great merchants and producers whose economic, social and political ambitions cannot in any sense be identified with those of the more humble people.

IV

The Influence of Humanist Thought on Christian Thought

When this civic freedom was achieved and consolidated, attention could turn again in the second half of the 15th century to those religious problems of early humanism.[20] The humanist search for classical manuscripts had brought to light many a treatise or collection of letters. This widened considerably the knowledge of various moral and religious systems, which could not fail to affect the exclusiveness of the Christian system. It had now to compete with Stoicism and Epicureanism and with ideas about divine revelation in the old religions of the world which preceded the revelation that took place in Christ within the Jewish community. And just as the 13th century saw the attempt at a Christian-Aristotelian synthesis, so efforts were now

[19] Cf. H. Baron, *The Crisis of the Early Italian Renaissance,* 2 vols. (Princeton, 1955), criticized by W. Ferguson and M. Seidlmayer, among others.

[20] E. Garin, in *Der italienische Humanismus* (Bern, 1947) stresses particularly the humanist outlook as the interpretation of man in active, "civic" life, but observes nevertheless that "if all Italian early humanism looks like a glorification of 'civic' life, of the freedom with which man builds an earthly state, then the end of the 15th century is marked by a clear tendency to flee from the world toward contemplation" (p. 92).

made to integrate all this new knowledge with Christian belief. This was more easily accomplished inasmuch as the new awareness of historical reality and the damage done to Thomism by the Church's condemnations had turned attention away from the speculative-dogmatic attitude of Christendom. Moreover, the realistic, pragmatic and rational approach of urban society was alien to that of the theologians and philosophers. Urban man tried to find his own expression of Christianity in the light of the historical discoveries of the humanists.

With his new open-mindedness, and lack of interest in dogma, man was sensitive to a concept of truth other than that of a naturalistic Aristotelianism. Petrarca, Boccaccio, Salutati and Ficino sensed poetically that the degree of reality of mythologies and poetry had something in common with that of biblical literature, and that there was no room here for the methods of formal logic. For these men the Bible was the greatest poem and theology was poetry about God. The figurative speech of pagan poets and religious thinkers agrees with the speech of Scripture, and all these texts veil one and the same truth, which the mind can approach but only love can seize. It is this truth that was fully manifested in Christ. Thus there is only one religion in a multiplicity of rites; to show this may finally dispose of all shedding of blood in the name of God and bring us closer to that harmony in the world [21] that lies implied in the dignity of man.

Another important element in this new mentality is that men begin to be capable of thinking historically. The Church and Christendom also underwent this new awareness of the historical processes, and the light falling on this history no longer showed it as a simple and straight development. People became aware of a whole spectrum of colors where, before, all had been uni-

[21] The most notable contribution in the north is Nicholas of Cusa, *De Pace Fidei*. See A. G. Weiler, *Nicolaas van Cues en de oecumenische problematiek vòòr de Reformatie* ('s-Hertogenbosch, 1964); B. Decker, "Nikolaus von Cues und der Friede unter den Religionen," in *Humanismus, Mystik und Kunst der Welt des Mittelalters*, ed. J. Koch (Leiden/Cologne, ²1959), pp. 94-121; M. Seidlmayer, " '*Una religio in rituum varietate.*' Zur Religionsauffassung des Nikolaus von Cues," in *Wege u. Wandlungen*, pp. 215-72.

formly white; all these elements had to be reconciled with the Christian truth and were already beginning to be so in principle. Without attacking Christianity as the final revelation of God, the Florentine thinkers tried to build up a harmonious philosophical synthesis of all the religious and moral systems of the world. There was no doctrinal controversy with Scholasticism, because the humanists in no way developed a new coherent theoretical system. But even in the discussion about God, the soul, providence, predestination, free will and immortality, they shifted the emphasis to the part played by man. Their dominating interest concerned itself with the understanding, justification and stimulating of *man's* free initiative in this world, as well as in the field of religion.

In this field historians distinguish two main features in Italian humanism.[22] There is, first of all, the recognition that religion also has a "civil" function to fulfill: the Bible also has a message for happiness on this earth, for a positive attitude toward labor, and it exhorts us to improve the world as a preparation for the communal life in heaven. Secondly, there are clear indications of at least the beginning of a theoretical tolerance. It is important to emphasize that the humanists did not think in terms of a peaceful coexistence between various religions by some recognition of the fact that the differences, such as they exist, are irreconcilable; the basis of their "ecumenical" efforts was the conviction that, within mankind, all forms of religious belief were basically one. The open approach of some of the Greek and Latin Fathers of the Church encouraged them in this view, and many humanists insist that *all* truth is from God.[23] God is the center of all that is, and therefore there is no such thing as being "nearer" or

[22] Abbagnano, *op. cit.*

[23] "All truth is from God. . . . Nothing is true outside God," wrote Colucc. Salutati to Fra Giovanni da S.Miniato. See Mestwerdt, *op. cit.*, pp. 37-38; M. Seidlmayer, "Relig.-eth. Probleme," p. 282; A. Renaudet, "Autour d'une définition de l'humanisme," p. 51. It is interesting that the Dutch New Catechism (*Nieuwe Katechismus*) (Hilversum, 1966) turns again to this line of thought in the discussion of world religions, with a reference to St. Thomas and St. Ambrose: *Omne verum, a quocumque dicatur, a Spiritu sancto est* (pp. 35, 36, 43).

"farther away". All religious systems start from the one truth, are radiations from the one sun, and culminate in Christ's revelation.

For some of these thinkers this led to a universalist idea of religion. They studied not only the "theologian-poets" of Greek and Roman antiquity, but also the Chaldaeans, Parsees, Indians, Egyptians and even the Jewish Kabbala with this one philosophical and comprehensive religion in mind, which can be harmonized with Christianity. This universalist tendency also influenced their moral views. Impressed by the human values of the non-Christian systems of morality, the humanists showed a similar attempt to reconcile Christian and non-Christian morality, with an inclination to adapt the former to the latter. In this process Christian morality lost that claim to absolute and exclusive validity which was based on the Church's authoritative interpretation of Christian revelation, since revelation itself had become universalist by then. This new moral view was not based on the faith in the strict and exclusive sense but on a dialogue between the faith and the historical manifestations of non-Christian idealized views of man. Christian teaching and its practical demands as formulated until then were pushed into the background, and only the pure Gospel (which meant also "pure" according to the method of philological criticism) could provide the norms for the new undogmatic, unsystematic inner life of man as a free, morally conscious person, responsible for himself.

These last remarks show perhaps the most characteristic feature of the religious and moral tendencies of humanism. These new men no longer sought contact with the theological and philosophical systems within the Church. They showed great aversion to that Aristotelian Scholasticism which, with its harsh methods of conceptual analysis, claimed to be able to give an exact rational definition of the contents of a closed system of faith and morality and to propose all this to people's belief with the authority of a schoolmaster.[24] This could hardly inspire a Christian commitment, particularly since it was out of touch with that new hu-

[24] Seidlmayer, *art. cit.*, pp. 291-2.

manist thought which permeated the concrete environment of a Christian's life in this world.

Putting this into modern terms one might say that the essentialist and universalist approach of Scholasticism no longer corresponded to the newly-understood existential needs of a society which had become urban, civically conscious, and articulate through humanist influence, and to the needs of the powerful, individualistic elite that was in control.[25] This disintegration of the traditional binding force of the old authority had, of course, frequently unfortunate results. Religious indifference, a definite paganism or anti-Church attitudes were unintended consequences of this new approach to the problem of religion. But there were also very positive results which led theology and its influence on Christian practice into new ways. The introduction of the scientific methods of literary criticism, philology and history into theology helped to free it from being enslaved to a system and led it back to the original sources of Christian belief: Scripture, the apostolic tradition, the Fathers and the councils of the first centuries. With the new editions of old manuscripts it helped to clear away the obscurities that had accumulated in the intervening period. There was a strong inclination to ignore the age of Scholasticism with its barbaric language and hair-splitting syllogisms, and to return to early Christianity with its cultural purity, the writings of the Fathers, its nearness to the Gospel and the active general consensus of the believing community when ecclesiastical regulations had to be drawn up.

v

THE HUMANISM OF THE NORTHERN COUNTRIES

This constructive tendency worked in favor of the old Church, particularly through the humanism of the northern countries.[26]

[25] A. G. Weiler, "Humanisme en scholastiek in de Renaissance-tijd," in *Annalen Thijmgenootschap* 51 (1963), pp. 307-34, with a summary in French.

[26] L. Spitz, *The Religious Renaissance of the German Humanists* (Cam-

The spiritual climate of northwestern Europe had been prepared by the personalized, practical piety of the *Devotio Moderna* which, with its aversion to mystical speculations and systematic theology, had emphasized the personal imitation of Christ in good works and virtuous living. This tendency toward a more inward religious life and the emphasis on the importance of the human will in this regard corresponded to the moral elements in Italian humanism. The methods of scientific philology, which the humanists had developed in order to enjoy their classical authors in the purest possible form, were here applied to the beloved sources of Christian piety, the Bible and the Fathers, partly on the lines worked out by Lorenzo Valla.[27] Thus this northern humanism first of all encouraged a more biblical and patristic reorientation of Christian life. This found expression in an experimental lay theology, clearly distinguished from the legalism and logical procedure of Scholasticism. All this was also penetrated by Florentine Platonism and here and there brought about a relativization of the absolute character of priesthood and dogma, and a spiritualization of the sacraments, particularly in people like Konrad Celtis, Johannes Reuchlin and Mutianus Rufus.

In general, one may say that while the data of revelation were not done away with, the emphasis fell on a will and moral action guided by the inner presence of God. The ideal was no longer a religion of obedience that thrived on a childlike acceptance of autonomous divine or ecclesiastical laws or truths imposed on man from outside. This attitude no longer paid any special atten-

---

bridge, Mass., 1963). Enno van Gelder's *The Two Reformations in the 16th Century. A Study of the Religious Aspects and Consequences of Renaissance and Humanism* (The Hague, ²1964) must be handled with caution as the sources are not always reliable and the author is inclined to make the humanists say more than they actually did. For example, Erasmus' intention is said to be "to *repel* in Christianity the idea of supernatural redemption by Christ's death on the cross and to lay *all* emphasis on what Christ preaches . . . on a virtuous life" (p. 140).

[27] E. F. Rice, Jr., "The Humanist Idea of Christian Antiquity: Lefèvre d'Etaples and His Circle," in *Studies in the Renaissance* 9 (1962), pp. 126-160. There is an appendix of the patristic editions published by Lefèvre d'Etaples and his circle, 1499-1520.

tion to the institutional aspects of the Church, her organization and her authoritative pronouncements, but rather to a religious inclination which has its source within man himself. Erasmus' *Enchiridion militis christiani* has been appropriately called the humanist's *Introduction à la vie dévote*.[28] In his environment the call for a more religious Church, a less superstitious worship, a more evangelical spirituality and a theology that concentrates more on the Word of God became the clearest formulation of the demands of Christian humanism. The evangelism of so many medieval reform movements was provided with new dimensions and new methods by this humanism. And this commitment to a Christian renewal went hand in hand with an increasingly radical opposition to the prevailing ways of thinking which, like flamboyant weeds, obscured the original simplicity of the Church. In this northern humanism the method of philological criticism and the moral criticism of ecclesiastical institutionalism, ecclesiastical science and ecclesiastical practice went hand in hand.

This movement ended up, partly, in a new reformed Church, detached from Rome. But it also remained partly active within this Church in the gentle figures of the Counter-Reformation. In both denominations it represented the "elastic" principle of tolerance and religious peace.

VI

CONCLUSION

As the expression of a newly acquired freedom, the humanism of the Renaissance embodied the ideology of man on the way toward human emancipation. This emancipation process almost reached its climax after the French Revolution, the two World Wars and the industrial and technological revolutions of modern times. The scientific, mathematical and electronic control of

[28] L. E. Halkin, "La 'Devotio Moderna' et les origines de la Réforme aux Pays-Bas," in *Courants religieux et humanisme à la fin du XVe et au début du XVIe siècles* (Paris, 1959), p. 51, with ref. to J. Dagens.

the world has put man in a situation of supreme self-determination, and his historical awareness has made him acutely conscious of the implied dangers. Paternalism is no longer tolerable and there is no longer room for it as a social function. Man decides his own destiny.

Will he remember the significance of a humanism which holds that the harmony of the universe can only be achieved through the inner personal morality of each individual? Christianity will gain nothing by ignoring the humanism of today. The present humanists are born of that same Christianity but, having acquired a new human existence, they have shaken off parental dogmatism, the cult of authority and the compulsion of the system. In their eyes these elements are real obstacles to the religious peace which they demand, like their parents, for the salvation of all mankind. To drop the barriers of orthodoxy is not necessarily in conflict with a genuine evangelical Christianity. The origin of this religious and moral humanism shows that it has a function to fulfill within the Church. Only a genuine dialogue can show how the specific Christian key points of human sin, divine grace and redemption in Christ can be maintained in unbroken continuity.[29]

[29] Cf. M. Seidlmayer, "Rel.-eth. Probleme," p. 294.

Adel-Théodore Khoury / *Münster, W. Germany*

The Byzantine Church and the Muslim World after the Fall of Constantinople

On May 29, 1453, Constantinople fell to the troops of Sultan Mahomet II. The patriarch, Gregory Mammas, had withdrawn to Rome because of the growing hostility of the Orthodox to the idea of reunion with the Roman Church. The emperor, Constantine XI, had died bravely in battle. The Byzantine Church had thus lost the two leaders who, by close collaboration, had provided stable ecclesiastical administration and at the same time had looked to the external prosperity of Christianity in the Eastern empire. The hope that a restoration movement might take root in other Byzantine centers was cruelly destroyed when Mistra in Morea (May 30, 1460) and Trebizond in Asia Minor (August 15, 1461) surrendered in quick succession.

I

CONSTERNATION

Despite all the signs which for years had been pointing to the final disaster, Christians of both East and West were so dismayed by the fall of the capital that they were moved to tears by its sad fate. The numerous lamentations written at the time draw attention to the many different aspects of the catastrophe. George

47

Scholarios, among others, deplored the material losses, the moral horrors, the ruins in which religion lay and the disappearance of Hellenic culture which marked the fall of Constantinople. With great sadness he admitted: "All this has happened because of our sins." [1] Doukas proclaimed the guilt of the people of Constantinople and implored the mercy of God for the sinners.[2] Latins and Uniate Greeks made it quite plain that they regarded the misfortune that had befallen the empire's capital as a punishment of the Orthodox people for their obstinacy in remaining in schism.[3]

II

REACTION

However, such interpretations of the reasons for the disaster did not satisfy everyone. Some reacted with a vigor that varied between the two extremes of open hostility to the conquerors and a desire to seek a reconciliation of principles, or syncretism, that would bring unity to the universe. On the other hand, the more realistic reaction dictated by circumstances varied between weak opportunism and prudent moderation, with an intermediate stage of various shades of liberalism.

The hostility of the Byzantines to Islam is clearly indicated in the short accounts devoted to their conquerors' religion. A biographical study of Mahomet is equaled for sheer fancifulness only by the account of the monk Bartholomew of Edessa (13th century).[4] Chalcocondyles, who makes a few observations on the law and doctrine of Islam, appears to have gathered his information from his personal contacts with various Muslims. But

[1] P.G. 160, pp. 263-4, n. 2.
[2] *Histoire turco-byzantine,* ed. Becker (Bonn, 1834), p. 311.
[3] *Chronicon majus* (Melissenos 1573-1575), ed. Becker (Bonn, 1838), pp. 310-12; P.G. 156, pp. 897-8.
[4] P.G. 158, pp. 1077-80. On Bartholomew of Edessa, see my work *Les théologiens byzantins et l'Islam* I, (Münster, 1966), pp. 261-95; for his life of Mahomet, cf. P.G. 104, pp. 1417-44.

the anecdotal nature of the information included and the willful carelessness with which he presents it in a haphazard and disjointed *exposé* indicate the historian's aversion for Islam, despite the equivocal manner of the article.[5]

While the historians kept within the bounds imposed by considerations of prudence, the politicians for their part directed all their energies to preparing the way for liberation. Their attention turned quite naturally to the Latin West, all the more so because those among them who were able to move freely were protagonists of ecclesiastical union with Rome who had for the most part sought refuge in Italy. They stressed the urgent need for a great crusade that would liberate Constantinople and remove the menace presented by the Ottoman armies which now hung over Italy and the entire West. Cardinal Bessarion, from Trebizond, wrote to the doge of Venice, Francesco Foscari (July 13, 1453), and later to the Italian princes, exhorting them to combine their energies and act in a noble cause.[6] Janus Lascaris turned to Charles V, conveying to him secret messages from the Greeks who were ready to rise up in revolt against their conquerors and to lead the war of liberation, on condition that their efforts were supported by the armies of the Christian West.[7] Others, including Aristoboulos Apostoles (called Arsenios) and Mark Mousouros, added their authority to the popes' calls for a crusade. All hope proved to be in vain, however, and the Byzantines were forced to conclude that the West had finally lost all interest in Constantinople.

Another group of Byzantines refused at the outset to engage in a political struggle with the Muslim Turks, believing it more sensible to try to persuade Sultan Mahomet II to accept some sort of syncretism by which the principles of both sides could be

---

[5] *Historiarum Demonstrationes* I ed. E. Darko (Budapest, 1922), pp. 112-18.

[6] Cf. H. Vast, *Le cardinal Bessarion (1403-1472)* (Paris, 1878), pp. 454-6; P.G. 161, pp. 641-76.

[7] Cf. E. Legrand, *Bibliographie hellénique* I (Paris, 1885); Borje Knös, *Un ambassadeur de l'Hellénisme, Janus Lascaris, et la tradition gréco-byzantine dans l'humanisme français* (Uppsala-Paris, 1945), pp. 186-91.

reconciled. George of Trebizond (born in Crete in 1395, died in Rome in 1484), for instance, sought to bring Mahomet II to Italy and convince him that it was his providential mission to achieve the political unity of the world with himself as supreme ruler, to put the seal on the ecclesiastical union of East and West, and, finally, to bring about the religious union of Christianity and Islam. As early as July, 1453, two months after the fall of Constantinople, George sent the sultan a treatise on "the truth of the Christian religion",[8] which treatise we now summarize.

After some magnificent expressions of praise for the prince, the author states that God has destined Mahomet II to rule over the universe (95-96). An obstacle to the fulfillment of his destiny is presented by the division separating Muslim and Christian princes; this division is founded, however, on ignorance on both sides, on a fondness for chicanery and on vanity, and not on religious doctrine (97-99). The doctrinal differences between Christianity and Islam can, in fact, be reduced to three main points: the Trinity, the incarnation, and the crucifixion and resurrection of Christ. Misunderstanding on these points can be resolved by careful analysis. The Trinity is not a negation of monotheism, for God is one in three persons (analogy with the sun, fire, the three-dimensional body). The dogma of the incarnation affirms the divinity of Christ and also his humanity, on which the Koran places great emphasis. The Old Testament bears testimony to these mysteries, and the Koran itself, in speaking of Christ, calls him the Word and the Spirit of God (Koran 4, 171). Finally, the philosophic teaching of Aristotle enables us to elucidate these dogmas in a satisfactory manner (Trinity: 100-132; Divinity of Christ: 132-149). As far as the death and resurrection of Christ (149-161) are concerned, there would seem to be an irresolvable contradiction between the statements in the Koran and the accounts to be found in the gospels. But the prophets of the Old Testament proclaim the death of Christ and thus confirm the gospels. Moreover, there is no reason why we should reject the possibility of Christ's death. It must therefore

[8] Ed. G. T. Zoras, *George of Trebizond* (Athens, 1954), pp. 93-165.

be concluded that the verse in the Koran (Koran 4, 157) is either a falsification or simply an interpolation. In any case, the law of the Muslims says that Christ will die at the end of time. Christ's death is thus recognized by both religions, even if it is placed at different dates. As for belief in the resurrection, this is to be found among all peoples.

George adds a paragraph in justification of the veneration of the cross and of icons (161), and then concludes that agreement between Christianity and Islam is total, except for the question of the death of Christ on the cross (162-163).

The treatise ends with a tirade in which the prince is exhorted to fulfill the role that has been assigned to him. Like Constantine, whom he surpasses in birth, in wisdom, in bodily strength and in spiritual energy, Mahomet II must accept the call of God and serve the interests of Christ (163-165).

This treatise, despite its interest, is superficial and unconvincing. George did not know Arabic and had an inadequate and fragmentary knowledge of Islam. He minimized the differences of dogma separating Islam from Christianity without supporting his theses with valid demonstrations. However, carried away by his own opinions, he embarked on a dangerous policy. He even set off a little later for Constantinople (November, 1465-March, 1466), where he established friendly relations with the sultan and provided him with political information concerning Italy. Mahomet II showered handsome gifts upon him, but he showed considerably less interest in his literary projects. Before returning to Italy George wrote the sultan two more letters (February 15 and March 18, 1466) in a last attempt to win his favor and obtain financial assistance from him. In these letters he returned to his ideas on the providential destiny of Mahomet II as the successor to the emperors of Byzantium. He also sent the sultan a Latin translation of the treatise of 1453 which has been analyzed above.[9]

[9] Cf. A. Mercati, "Le due lettere di Giorgio da Trebisonda a Maometto II," in *Orientalia Christiana Periodica* (1943), pp. 65-99; text of the letters: I, pp. 85-92; II, pp. 92-99.

George of Trebizond gained few disciples and a great many enemies. His tribulations, together with disillusionment, brought him to a more realistic view of things. On April 23, 1468 he wrote the *Passion* of the martyr Andrew of Chios[10] who had been executed by the Muslims in Constantinople on May 29, 1465.

Andrew of Chios was not the only one to seal his fidelity to Christ with his blood; many others, especially in the early days of the Muslim conquest, had to die for their faith. One must remember yet another great trial which afflicted the Byzantine Church over a long period: the conversion, either voluntary or enforced, of Christians to the religion of their new masters. The *Passion* of Andrew of Chios mentions the conversion to Islam of a peripatetic philosopher from Trebizond; whether the conversion was sincere or dictated by circumstances, the author is unwilling to say. He does not even name the person in question.[11] Some have identified him as George Amirutzes. On the fall of Trebizond (August 15, 1461) Amirutzes had been deeply grieved by the deportation of his son who, he wrote, "is virtuous and has not betrayed his paternal glory" (i.e., the faith of his forefathers).[12] But it would appear that, subsequently, Amirutzes himself was not able to resist the pressure of circumstances, for he went over to Islam and put himself at the service of the sultan.[13]

The defection of Amirutzes was not an isolated case. The Church was to grieve over many similar defections. Her most painful ordeal, however, was the compulsory enlistment of large numbers of young people, a human "tithe" exacted for the purpose of recruiting Janissaries. These boys, taken away by force and brought up in the Muslim faith under the strictest discipline, formed the elite of the Ottoman army. In words touched with emotion Janus Lascaris describes the "miserable fate of the child

[10] P.G. 161, pp. 883-90.
[11] *Ibid.*, I, p. 883B.
[12] Letter to Bessarion: P.G. 161, p. 727A-B. We also possess a dialogue between Amirutzes and Mahomet on Christianity, ed. J. Werner (Nürnberg, 1514).
[13] Cf. E. Legrand, *op. cit.*, III (Paris, 1903), pp. 195-205.

snatched from the arms of his protesting mother to be taken elsewhere and there made to accept a law contrary to the law of
Jesus Christ and to serve the tyrants of some ministry or other;
these boys end up by engaging in war against their own fathers
and kinsfolk".[14]

Not all opportunists were converted to Islam. A great many
Christians sought to gain the sultan's favor by putting their
literary talents or technical knowledge at his service. Critoboulos
of Imbros, for example, devoted a *History* in five volumes to the
exploits of Mahomet II from 1450 to 1467.[15]

III

COLLABORATION

This kind of collaboration with the new regime indicated a
certain relaxation of hostility in men's minds. Circumstances
called for modification on some durable basis of the Christian
attitude to the new political conditions. A change of attitude had
already been initiated shortly after the fall of Constantinople.
Sultan Mahomet II himself, by showing a highly conciliatory
spirit, made it easier for people to contain their animosity. He
intervened personally to hasten the election of the new patriarch
of Constantinople. He attended the investiture of George Scholarios (who took the name of Gennadios II), presented him with
a precious scepter, bestowed countless gifts upon him and had
him mount a richly harnessed horse and ride with escort through
the city to his patriarchal residence.[16] He granted Scholarios a
firman (act of official recognition) establishing him at the head
of the "Greek nation": the patriarch thus became the religious
and civil leader of his flock. The general provisions of Muslim

[14] Letter to Charles V in E. Legrand, *op. cit.,* I. On the recruitment
of Janissaries, cf. F. Babinger, *Mehmed der Eroberer und seine Zeit*
(Munich, 1953), pp. 472-73.

[15] Ed. C. Müller, *Fragmenta Historicorum graecorum* V (Paris, 1883).

[16] He was imitating the practice of the *basileus;* cf. L. Bréhier, *Les
institutions de l'empire byzantin* (Paris, 1949), pp. 479-81.

law gave Christians the political protection of the State and the freedom to practice their religion and to be governed in religious and judicial matters by their own religious leaders, each according to his personal status. Mahomet II even granted certain privileges to the patriarch and his priests. The position of Christians was consequently that of the *dhimmis* or tributaries of Islam, who had to pay for their relative freedom by submitting to various poll taxes and other contributions to the State treasury.

If, in theory, the government guaranteed its support to the religious leaders of the Greek people, in practice the sound administration of the Church, religious peace and the respecting of the rights and privileges granted depended not only on the law, but also on the political conditions of the time, on the climate of relations with other Christian nations, on the favor of the sultan and on the good humor of viziers and various other officials. The court insisted on selling its favors at a price, and as a result corruption opened the door to simony and, with simony, to disastrous rivalries among the claimants to the patriarchal see; this naturally led to instability in the administration of the Church.[17] What is more, though the authority of the patriarch, as the sole officially recognized leader, was being established on the administrative and civil plane, the center of gravity of the Byzantine Church was, in fact, shifting toward Greece. After the massacres and deportations that followed the fall of the city, Constantinople was never again to attain the original density of its Christian population. Byzantine Christendom ebbed back to Greece, where it strove to preserve its cultural heritage and its religious vitality and to encourage hope of political liberation.

IV

THE DOCTRINAL POSITION OF THE CHURCH

In the meantime, the Church had to take a position with regard to Islam in the field of doctrine. It was essential that the

[17] Cf. R. Janin, "Constantinople," in *Dict. Hist. Géogr. eccl.* 13 (Paris, 1956), pp. 675-80.

faithful should be warned to guard against the temptations of defection and that the Christian faith should be defended against the objections of the Muslims. This task now fell more and more to the clergy. The patriarch, Gennadios (Scholarios), even had occasion to draw up an apologia of Christianity at the request of Mahomet II and to reply to various objections made by Ottoman pashas. We know that the Muslim conquerors were in the habit of consulting the religious leaders of tributary nations about their respective systems of law, so that their flocks might continue to be governed under that same law.

The sultan had three conversations with the patriarch. After the second meeting he asked Scholarios to put the basic doctrines of his *exposé* in writing. Scholarios then composed the document entitled "Concerning the Sole Path Leading to Salvation".[18] In it he explained the succession of the three laws—natural, written (Mosaic) and evangelical. Christianity, Scholarios wrote, is the final fruition of the Old Testament, of ancient wisdom and pagan prophecy. The Christian law is the perfect and definitive law; no law coming after it and contradicting it in any way can be considered divine. Finally, if there are schisms among Christians, this is due not to the existence of several gospels, but to the diverse interpretations of the sacred texts.

The sultan found the *exposé* difficult to understand and asked the patriarch to draw up a clearer text. Scholarios then wrote his "Confession of Faith" [19] in which he attempted to elucidate the mysteries of faith with the help of various analogies—the Trinity (fire, the human soul), the incarnation (union of soul and body). The last paragraph deals with the grounds of credibility: the prophetic proclamation of the coming of Christ (Old Testament, Greek oracles, Greek and Persian astronomers and various other prophecies), the agreement to be found among the Scriptures, the wonderful way in which Christianity had spread, the sublimity of the Christian law, miracles, the strength of doc-

[18] *Oeuvres complètes* III, éd. Petit-Sidéridès-Jugie (Paris, 1930), pp. 434-52. On the spurious matter published in P.G. 160, pp. 319-32, cf. M. Jugie, *ibid.*, XXXI-XXXIV.
[19] *Ibid.*, pp. 453-58.

trine which triumphs over all objections and, finally, the perseverance of Christians under persecution.

Later (end of May, 1470), in the city of Serrai, after his third resignation, Scholarios had another discussion on the divinity of Christ with two pashas.[20] Once again he enumerated the grounds of credibility which militate in favor of Christianity and replied to the objections of his interlocutors.

These texts give no hint of the excesses of language and the bitter polemics which for centuries had marked Byzantine writings on Islam.[21] The Byzantines, subjected now to the Ottoman sultan, had on the whole to be content with a firm apologetic of the Christian faith conducted in a conciliating tone but without doctrinal concessions. After the extremes of angry hostility and reckless enthusiasm that had characterized the early days of Ottoman rule, the Byzantine Church was compelled to adapt herself to her position of *dhimmi* or tributary within the Muslim State. In the hope of better days to come she directed her energies to the preservation of the faith and religious vitality of her flock and to the preservation of the Greek language, which constituted a bond both cultural and national.

It was this flame, hidden for many centuries beneath ashes, that one day enabled the Hellenic Church of Byzantium to rise again with the advent of an independent Greece and to look to the future through eyes eager with all the hope that had been so patiently kept burning.

[20] *Ibid.,* pp. 458-75.
[21] Cf. my *Polémique byzantine contre l'Islam* (Münster, 1966).

Reinerus Post/*Nijmegen, Netherlands*

The Church on the Eve of the Reformation

In 1517, when Luther proclaimed his then startling opinions about the meaning of certain texts in St. Paul, particularly in the letter to the Romans, and made some important dogmatic and pastoral statements, the Church was a shrunken Church. For 500 years the Christians of Asia and Africa no longer belonged to the Church of Rome, apart from a few insignificant exceptions. The Catholic Church had become a European Church, and the Church of a small Europe at that, because the Russians had joined the Eastern Church and the Balkans and Spain were under Islamic power. Moreover, in southern Europe the outlook was dark because the Ottoman Turks exercised increasing pressure on the northwest, threatening not only Hungary, but even Austria and, at certain moments, Italy. The attempts of a few kings to stem this invasion were often lacking in power and had little success outside Spain. The threat to central Europe was real and the source of constant worry to popes and emperors.

More encouraging were the reports sent by missionaries from the countries in Asia, Africa and America which had just been opened up and were within easy reach. However, these newly-founded Churches demanded a great deal of care in their formative years and needed support and protection. This led to some necessary administrative measures which, in turn, led to new problems about the relations between Church and State in Spain and Portugal. That these missionary successes in the newly-discovered regions counterbalanced the losses sustained in Europe is an optical illusion of a later age. In the age of Luther and early Protestantism the leaders of the Catholic Church could hardly see the missionary successes as making up for the damage done at home. The small size of the Church only added to the seriousness of what was lost through the Reformation. The secession of the Churches of Denmark, Norway, Sweden, England, Scotland, Prussia and large sections of Germany, Switzerland and Hungary weakened the existing Catholic Church still further.

At the same time important changes took place in the secular sphere which undermined the existing powers and reduced them to impotence for a time. The trade picture was completely changed as a result of new passages by sea, vast new regions, a discredited feudalism and the rise of capitalism in commerce, mining, printing and industry; this transformed the image of the world, stimulated observation and experiment, and cast doubt on the old knowledge about nature, both vegetable and animal. All this reinforced the demand, already formulated for some time, for a reform of the Church and religious practice.

If it is true that the later Middle Ages looked forward to a more genuinely religious Church, a less superstitious worship, a more evangelical spirituality and a theology that was more clearly founded on the Word of God, then Luther hit the nail on the head with his ninety-five theses which he affixed to the doors of the church in Wittenberg on October 31, 1517. The preaching of indulgences was seen by many as a contradiction of evangelical spirituality, a too easy way of securing spiritual benefits, and even as a relaxation of morality and a devout life. It could easily be branded as not in agreement with the Gospel. Moreover, some theologians, such as Wessel Gansfort, had denied even before Luther the foundation of this teaching about indulgences, the existence of a so-called "treasury of the Church" gathered from the merits of Christ and the saints, or they had given this expression a very different interpretation.

Although drafted in Latin, some of Luther's theses were aimed at the general public. Some sounded rebellious, such as those about the "treasury of the Church". According to Luther the pope was wealthier than Croesus, so he did not need the money derived from indulgences. Luther thought that indulgences should be preached in a manner very different from that used by those who preached in Saxony and elsewhere. Sermons should aim at the renewal of man. They should be penitential, which they were in theory but not in practice, as Luther knew from experience. In fact, such preaching no longer fitted in with Luther's opinion of the way in which man could attain salvation. This opinion, which was new, was easily felt as more biblical and less superficial and formalistic than the obtaining of letters of indulgence. If it did not include man's penance the indulgence barely touched the inner religious life at all.

The fact is that these theses appealed very much to the people. They spread all over Germany, both in Latin and in German. Various printers of note cooperated to satisfy the general demand. And so Luther, until then an unknown professor of a small new university, became famous overnight. He had touched a particularly sensitive nerve—the desire for a more fervent piety, which I mentioned above. Perhaps it was even more important that he had appealed to the anti-Roman mood which prevailed in Germany. The first result was the most primitive reaction, namely, opposition to any payment of money to Rome, to which the Germans were particularly averse as is clear from the formulation of the *gravamina nationis Germanicae,* the grievances of the German nation. In 1456 the assembly of German princes at Frankfurt had made these their own for the first time. Usually reasserted at the following diets, they became a means of anti-Roman agitation.

One cannot ignore this anti-Roman mood when dealing with the religious attitude of the late Middle Ages. Within the empire many were convinced that this money, sent from the empire to Rome, was spent superfluously on what seemed to them vast and luxurious churches and palaces, or even on the wealthy and scandalous lives of ecclesiastical authorities. It was thought that these finances served to pay the troops used for the territorial Italian policies of the Papal States and to support the relatives of some of the popes, and this meant sometimes even against the interests of the empire. Moreover, several Germans were convinced (and not without reason) that they contributed far more to the curia and its institutions than the inhabitants of other European countries. They thought that the reduced power of the emperor and the central government weakened their possible resistance to the financial demands made by the Roman authorities, when compared with other European kings. In the 14th century England already had its Statutes of Provisors (1344) and the Statute of Praemunire (1377) which enabled the king to check papal nominations for prebends and ecclesiastical posts in England and the accompanying payment of *servitia* and annates to Rome. The king could even keep Italians out of England if they appeared as papal legates. Under Henry VIII this far-reaching power was in the hands of an Englishman, Thomas Wolsey, which, however, did not prevent the Italian Campeggio from functioning by his side in "the king's matter", the divorce he contemplated.

The French Church had practically been handed over to the king by the Pragmatic Sanction of Bourges in 1438, and particularly since the Concordat of 1515 with Francis I. The king, in fact, made all appointments to bishoprics and abbeys. This did not in fact stop all payments to Rome but the kings made sure that the rich revenues of the French Church did not easily flow out of the country. The Spanish throne, too, especially Ferdinand and Isabella, extended its power over the Church as they extended it over the peninsula. They protected ecclesiastical revenue against the claims of the curia and managed to acquire the disposal of the revenues of the wealthy Spanish orders of knights. How the Burgundians and Austrians acquired the Dutch and Flemish bishoprics of Liège, Cambrai, Terwaan, Tournai and Utrecht for their families is well known. The payment of *servitia*, although not excluded by this maneuver, was nevertheless greatly diminished because the princes themselves nominated some of the lower ecclesiastical functionaries.

The powerful German princes, such as the Duke of Bavaria, pursued on their own the same policy as the emperor, but the ecclesiastical electorates of Mainz, Trier and Cologne and most other bishoprics maintained free elections. However, those elected needed confirmation by the pope and, with that, committed themselves to the payment of high *servitia*. In spite of the free election, only members of the higher aristocracy were chosen, partly because the electors belonged themselves to this aristocracy, but especially because the ecclesiastical princes needed the support of the other princes. Moreover, these ecclesiastical principates had a powerful attraction for the higher nobility.

The cooperation between princes and high ecclesiastical functionaries was another important aspect of the late medieval Church. When it came to taxing ecclesiastical revenue, secular and ecclesiastical officials often worked together. To make it possible for a prince to go on a crusade, particularly to fight the Turks in the Balkans, the pope repeatedly allowed the king, duke or count to levy a tithe on all ecclesiastical revenues for one or more years. Especially in the traffic of indulgences, delegates of Church and State worked hand in hand. The princes allowed the preachers into their territory only on condition that they could pocket part, often one-third, of the proceeds. This kind of thing happened, for instance, with the notorious indulgence proclaimed for the building of St. Peter's in 1516. Charles V allowed this indulgence to be preached in his Dutch territories on condition that he would be given one-third of the revenue. He then proposed to use this money for the building or strengthening of the dykes (the "dyke" indulgence). In the same way the elector of Mainz was to receive a percentage of the proceeds which he had to use in order to pay Rome the *servitia* of the dioceses of Magdeburg and Halberstadt, which had been assigned to him apart from the electorate. This cooperation, based on a compromise, often tied the representative of the Church completely to the State, with the result that it was difficult for him to introduce reforms if the prince of the territory was opposed to them. On the other hand, he often could use a neighboring prince's troops and power for ecclesiastical purposes, which, on occasion, increased the power of the inquisition and sometimes led to tyranny.

In some ways the late medieval Church returned to the situation that had prevailed in the 11th century: a subjection of the Church and Church officials to secular princes, or even the lower nobility and urban corporations. Actually the bishops had little or no influence on the choice, appointment and training of parish priests, curates and all kinds of vicars. The supervision of such persons by the bishop meant little since he was powerless against the patrons who had appointed them. That is why Luther's creation of so-called "Landeskirchen" (territorial churches under a secular authority) in Germany was not a far-reaching novelty: it had been prepared during the preceding age. The lords of the land were already accustomed to administering much of the Church in their own territory, and the clergy had become more or less accustomed to this situation.

A third aspect of the Church on the eve of the Reformation also came to the fore with the nailing of Luther's theses to the church doors—the question of papal authority. After the exaggerations of the 13th century, the 14th inevitably brought a reaction which became particularly articulate during the Councils of Constance and Basle, and later in many controversial and canonical writings. The attack on the indulgences immediately brought out the question of papal authority, and this soon became more important and more complex than that of the indulgences. Sources for this fact are many: the letter Luther wrote to Leo X, with an analysis and defense of his opinions; the letter written by Sylvester Prierias, the papal theologian; Luther's discussion with Cardinal Cajetan at Augsburg; the dispute of Leipzig; the condemnation in Rome and at the Diet of Worms. Luther was fully aware of the importance of this element. Because of this, in his *An den christlichen Adel deutscher Nation von des christlichen Standes Besserung,* he called on the emperor, the princes and the nobility to take over the reform of the Church since the pope and the bishops had neglected it. Luther's friend, von Hütten, aired his national hatred of Rome in his pamphlet *Vadiscus seu trias Romana*. This may be the language of an over-sensitive and poetic nature, but the doubt and denial of the plenitude of papal authority was older, and it was alive else-where: in Wycliffe and his followers in England, the Hussites in Bohemia, the Gallicans in France, Wessel Gansfort in Holland.

Can we find the late medieval longing for a more religious Church, a less superstitious worship and a more biblical spiritu-ality in those ninety-five theses of Luther's? The longing is pres-ent at least in the passage where Luther demands that the preach-ing of indulgences should be such as to increase the devout life. When we understand the penance of which Luther speaks as a sense of sin, we shall understand him better, and not only him but also the theology of the later Middle Ages with which the sense of devotion is linked. This sense of piety and its dogmatic background need a little explanation. The sense of sin must lead to trust in Christ and totally exclude any meritorial value of one's own works.

This denial of merit to human works was completely opposed to the school of theology which goes by the name of William of Ockham, who had a large following in late medieval universities, though not everywhere in the same degree. There were those who followed Ockham's philosophical theory about cognition but not his opinion about the value of human deeds with which we are here concerned. In general his followers accepted that if one does what one is capable of, one can attain primary justice and merit eternal reward. According to them one can merit the first grace in the strict sense. Ockham and his followers also taught the absolute sovereignty of God, so that God could refuse the reward of heaven to someone who did his best and give it to someone of whom this can hardly be said. Whether the re-ward is granted or not depends not only on man's exertion but also on God's preparedness to accept or refuse it.

Thomas Aquinas and others introduced the necessary dis-tinctions into this question. But there were others who, in op-

position to Ockham, saw in any recognition of human actions as
meritorious a revival of Pelagianism, condemned by the Church.
One of these was Johannes Pupper van Goch, a priest of Utrecht,
who wrote his main work about 1473 as rector of a convent of
Malines. Unfortunately this was only found and published during the years of the Reformation. He called Thomas Aquinas a
Pelagian, and it is still difficult for some Protestant theologians
to believe that this was not true of Thomas and his disciples.
The influence of these theologians spread so far that we find
their theories in Luther: justice comes from Christ and only
through faith. This disregard of human activity fitted in with
the sovereignty of God, which led to the acceptance of a strict
view of predestination by some late medieval theologians. It is
obvious that these theories influenced religious practice both before and after the Reformation. The denial of any meritorious
value to human actions could lead to a lax moral life both in
the monasteries and outside, which is what in fact happened.
But the opposite view might lead to an overrating of oneself,
pride, boasting about religious feats and the exaggerated con-
centration on observance.

This "observantism" was typical of monastic life in the 15th
century and the beginning of the 16th. It was also partly a reaction to the rather general laxness in the following of monastic
rules and customs. This "observantism" was seen as an ideal
mainly by the four mendicant orders of Franciscans, Dominicans,
Carmelites and Augustinian Friars. But it appeared also among
some leaders of the older orders of Benedictines, Cistercians,
Norbertines and the Canons of St. Augustine, with their female
counterparts. Among the Canons of St. Augustine the Congregation of Windesheim, which covered a territory that corresponds
today to Western Germany and the Low Countries, saw in this
fostering and maintaining of observance one of its principal tasks
in life. Similar features appeared in Italy, France and Spain.

This movement was evidenced, among other things, in the
setting up of congregations within an order or in one or two
provinces of the order. These religious were convinced that the

strictness of monastic life was best served by their own authorities who would understand these ideals. Only such authorities could keep a close enough eye on this observance in a relatively small circle, and if necessary take whatever measures were required. It was a laudable effort, for the protagonists meant to take the statutes and intentions of their founders seriously and carry through the issues of personal poverty and the communal life. But it is curious to see with what drastic means they tried to achieve their ideals: the calling on the secular arm for assistance, the armed attacks on monasteries, the expulsion of a number of members (often without a pension for those who objected), the denigration of the past, and even the use of false reports. It was indeed a fierce conflict where the end seemed to justify the means.

Even Luther belonged to this movement for a time. When a representative of this group had to plead their cause in Rome, Luther was sent along with him. The central government of the Church tried to bring about a reconciliation. In fact, both groups had come somewhat closer to each other by the beginning of the 16th century because the more liberal-minded had agreed to apply the rules more strictly. Among the Franciscans, however, the attempt at reconciliation broke down completely in 1515; the same year saw unity restored among the Dominicans, while the Augustinians maintained a separate administration for the time being. Luther himself was given the rank of "vicar" on his return from Rome and put at the head of a group of monasteries that opted for "observance". He took this seriously and exercised his function responsibly, but it soon became clear (1515) that inwardly he had ceased to believe in this ideal. Some of his statements even show distaste for this kind of observantism. In his exegesis of the epistles of St. Paul he identified Paul's opposition to Jewish law with the too formalistic application of the monastic rules, constitutions and customs.

And was it not in fact this legalistic mentality that prevailed among Christians on the eve of the Reformation? Did they not make the devout life consist in precisely this observance of regulations, so that they even boasted of the quantity of their prayers and good deeds in order to collect treasures in heaven in that way? They, no doubt, did these good deeds with the good intention of honoring God and helping their neighbor, but was this their only intention? Was it not mixed up with other selfish intentions?

Accordingly, one of the most typical features of the religious mentality of the masses just before the Reformation was this overemphasis on outward actions and the lack of a truly inner life. The "Little Office" was sung in Latin, not only in the churches of monasteries and cathedral chapters, but also in the parish churches and even in small chapels. This "divine office" involved numerous people. When there were not enough priests, lay people took over, particularly on the main feasts in the smaller churches. These services lasted a long time. Processions, vigils and commemorations were added to the proper office. There was no end to the founding of vicariates, prebends and payments for the recitation of special prayers. Furthermore, there was never a lack of candidates who wanted such a vicariate, had themselves ordained priests and then led an easy though not too wealthy life ever after.

There was always much going on in the churches but genuine devotion was rare. The singing or reciting of Latin texts that were not understood did not satisfy the desire for genuine devotion. This was sought rather in individual prayers and exercises, and especially in pilgrimages. For these there was plenty of opportunity, not only at the great and well-known places of pilgrimage, but also in numerous other ones where specific saints were buried, or eucharistic miracles or apparitions had taken place, or where so-called miraculous statues drew vast numbers of faithful. Here they could at least satisfy their personal devotions. The long or constantly repeated prayers were alternated with hymns and music. The solemnities almost imperceptibly turned into fairs. The pilgrimage usually included confession and communion. For the rest, the reception of the sacraments was poor, even in the monasteries. Only on the four main feasts, called "communion days", was the church particularly busy.

There was great interest in the founding of monasteries, beguinages, almshouses, orphanages and lazarhouses. Towns were full of such institutions and it appears that, before the Reformation, there was never any shortage of novices. For a large part, these novices often found themselves there not as a matter of personal choice or even against their will; the fact of the matter was that many monasteries, particularly of the older orders, ran institutions where young people, mostly girls of large and especially noble families, were taken care of. There was, nevertheless, in the 15th century an undeniable desire for a stricter rule, particularly among the numerous tertiaries who first wanted to take binding vows and later asked for incorporation in the manner of the Carthusians.

In spite of all the good that was achieved and the many outlets for religious feeling, the faithful were still not satisfied; they wanted something better, a "reform in head and members" as the phrase went in those days. What direction should this reform take? What kind of spiritual forces could bring it about?

In these circumstances some radical, though moderate, demands were made. The movement of the *Devotio Moderna,* which sprang up in Deventer at the end of the 14th century under the leadership of a few groups of committed men and women, made a deeper and more inward religious life its confessed aim. This the members tried to achieve, not by abolishing all oral prayers and offices, but by using every silent moment of the day to withdraw within themselves and to meditate upon some aspect of Christ's life or suffering or upon the four last things. For this occupation they used the significant word *ruminare* (to ruminate). Some among them pursued the paths of mysticism which had been previously followed by J. Ruusbroec and some German mystics. The Congregation of Windesheim turned to that monastic "observance" mentioned above, and were followed from afar by the Brethren of the Common Life who were not averse to commemorations and vigils either. There were other groups of persons with similar ideals elsewhere, as in Prague before the condemnation of John Hus or in France under the influence of

Jean Gerson. It was not until later that the Utraquists (primarily, those who wanted communion under both kinds for the laity) appeared with more radical demands, such as no property or power for the clergy and the punishment of mortal sin by the secular authority.

Like Erasmus many were in favor of a simple worship. He himself never had a good word to say for ceremonies. He often expressed his dislike for them, as for instance in this adapted commentary on Psalm 14: "One does not obtain access to the temple by means of ceremonies or papal bulls,[1] but through the purified spirit of faith and the exercise of brotherly love.[2] We have a precious and devout worship and ritual. Some may rely on it without noticing the required purity of mind. Others spend a great deal on decorating the churches, founding altars and building monasteries, but they do not give to their poor neighbors, which is an obligation.[3] Some think they have reached the summit of devotion (*pietas*) when they have a Mass said in a certain place on a certain day, or a benediction in honor of Our Lady.[4] But what am I saying? Do I want to do away with outward worship? Far from it—but I would free it from superstition and restore devotion. I would like to stop the exaggerations and bring in some moderation and piety.[5] There is no point in obeying the formal regulations about fasting and hearing Mass if it does not lead to improvement." [6]

Many, particularly the humanists, objected to the way in which theology and philosophy were taught at the universities at the end of the Middle Ages. It made people neither better nor wiser. The followers of the "new way" attributed absolute power to God. This led to fruitless and foolish speculation. For them this meant that God could create anything humanly imaginable and not contradictory in itself outside the existing order. It was

[1] Erasmus, *Opera Omnia* V (Leiden, 1705), p. 301B.
[2] *Op. cit.*, V, p. 301B.
[3] *Op. cit.*, V, p. 309C.
[4] *Op. cit.*, V, p. 309D.
[5] *Op. cit.*, V, p. 309E.
[6] *Op. cit.*, V, p. 309F.

imaginable that in another world order other moral laws than the existing ones could be valid. In this way one could endlessly argue about all kinds of nonsensical problems, which some of them were already too much inclined to do. This, of course, led theology farther and farther away from the Bible and the patristic tradition, and so discredited the whole subject. Erasmus and his friends wanted a more biblical and religious way of observing theology. They also thought that philology should be brought into the study of Scripture. They therefore considered that Latin, Greek and Hebrew were essential to the theologian and that the humanist theologians should start with improving the then current texts.

These demands were moderate enough, but the Reformers went much further. Luther, for instance, in the work mentioned above (1520), denied the distinction between spiritual and secular power in the Church, between clergy and laity, and rejected the Church's exclusive claim to the interpretation of the Bible as well as the pope's exclusive claim to convoke councils. He rejected the Mass and the sacraments except three—baptism, confession and the eucharist; he denied that popes and prelates had the authority to impose certain obligations on the faithful, and soon after, in 1522, he rejected monastic vows, celibacy for the clergy, and the private Mass which the Augustinians of Wittenberg had already abolished some time before. All this was accepted in the Protestant regions. In an effort at reconciliation, various persons and authorities urged communion under both kinds and a married clergy.

One might see in this desire for improvement and reform perhaps the desire for a more personal contact with Christ through the Gospel, a religious practice that was more inward and based on Christ's precepts, a simpler and more biblical dogma and a limitation of ecclesiastical authority. Perhaps many followers of the Reformation, and certainly many that supported the Counter-Reformation, could be satisfied for the time being with such a very simple skeleton program, while what was good and beautiful in the cultural tradition could be maintained. In fact, however, much more was changed. The Reformers threw aside much more than what I have just mentioned: they emphasized their own dogma of the certainty of salvation based on "faith alone", the "scriptures alone". Calvinism did away in large part with the established worship, while maintaining the "service of the Word". They "cleansed" the churches and accepted strict predestination. They eliminated much that caused scandal, or limited it, such as the veneration of statues and relics and numerous places of pilgrimage.

This condition lasted a long time before the Catholic Church found enough spiritual strength to introduce the desired changes along broad lines. Only under Pope Paul III (1534-9) could one observe the first clear signs of a renewal—namely, when he set up a Commission of Cardinals in 1538 to draft suggestions for a renewal of the Church. This group contained men who were both able and ready to do so. But the Council of Trent only started in 1546. The old German hierarchy, with little theological training and wholly taken up by the administration of their principalities, were neither trained for nor instructed in this reform. Here and there the bishops were forced by secular princes, particularly the Duke of Bavaria, at least to inform themselves of the situation by means of visitations. In France, the bishops spent too much time at the royal court. In Italy some members of the hierarchy showed interest and a spirit of sacrifice, with Giberti, Bishop of Verona, as one of the pioneers. The measures discussed or taken by provincial or diocesan synods to improve the training of the lower clergy during the first half of the 16th century brought no change until the decree of Trent on the establishment of clerical training centers was applied, which only took place in the second half of that century. A great number of priests ignored celibacy, but many longed for a more religious life.

The new climate in Italy gave rise to new congregations and orders. Their members were dedicated clerics who adjusted their activity and spirituality to the new demands, such as the Theatines, Barnabites, Somaschi, the Italian Oratorians and especially the Jesuits. Nuns also sought to make themselves useful to society—for example, the Ursulines. Finally, the Council of Trent not only brought important dogmatic decisions but also measures for the improvement of pastoral care and the life of clergy and laity. However, it was difficult to abolish the privileges of special groups, such as the canons, since society was so totally built up on privilege. Here and there were powerful conservative reactions. In some southern countries, unfortunately, the spirit of the medieval inquisition revived.

All this means that the Church has constantly to take stock and readjust herself to those Christian ideals which come to the fore in any given age.

Henry Bernard-Maître, S.J./*Chantilly, France*

The Chinese
and Malabar Rites

It was only in the very last public sessions of its fourth meeting that Vatican Council II adopted the *Declaration on Non-Christian Religions* (*Nostra aetate*) and the *Declaration on the Church's Missionary Activity* (*Ad gentes*). The two documents had been the subject of much debate and controversy. *Nostra aetate* was adopted on October 28, 1965 with 2,221 in favor, 88 opposed and 3 abstaining. *Ad gentes* was adopted on the eve of the Council's closing, December 7, 1965, with 2,394 in favor and 5 opposed. These documents were promulgated within the general framework set up by the *Pastoral Constitution on the Church in the Modern World* (*Gaudium et spes*), which was promulgated on the last day, with 2,309 in favor, 75 opposed and 7 abstaining. There is no doubt that if these documents had been put to a vote at the beginning of the conciliar sessions, the opposing votes would have been much more numerous. For all practical purposes, most bishops had inherited the outlook of a Bossuet, for example, who felt that all men could be saved but only on an *individual* basis.[1]

[1] As far as *printed* books are concerned, the *Bibliotheca Missionum* of Streit and Didinger (Freiburg im Br.) is pretty exhaustive up to the date of its publication: Vol. V (1929), *Asia 1600-1699*, pp. 24-1114; Vol. VI (1931), *India 1700-1799*, pp. 1-238; *Indochina*, pp. 421-548; Vol. VII (1931), *China 1700-1799*, pp. 24-544.

As far as the countless *manuscripts* are concerned, we must mention

Schillebeeckx[2] has this to say about the *Declaration on Non-Christian Religions:*

Taken as a whole, the tone and the perspective of this document represents a new official outlook on the part of the Church. . . .

The Church respects the "religious experience" which forms the basis of non-Christian religions . . . and this statement marks the starting point for a new outlook on the believers of these religions, and for a sincere and prudent dialogue with them.

The Church's historic confrontation with other religions,

---

the ones we came across, as the occasion warrants. In Rome itself, outside of the Vatican Archives and those of Propaganda Fide and the National Library, three Cardinal libraries contain an immense but incompletely indexed file of documents: Angelia, Casanatense and Corsini. It was there that Norbert obtained materials for his *Mémoires historiques,* which was put on the Index by Benedict XIV but often republished. It seems that the fragments were reproduced faithfully enough, but they were chosen to prove a point. Other documents of importance, presenting the other side of the case, were appended to various chapters of Pastor's *History of the Popes,* which makes use of the best general treatment of "Chinese (Rites)", the article by J. Brucker in the *Dictionnaire de Théologie catholique.* This should be complemented by an article of the same title in the *Dictionnaire d'Histoire et de Géographie ecclésiastiques* XII (Paris, 1953), cols. 731-41, and by "La correspondance Becker-Brucker sur la question des rites chinois (1885-1907)," in *Recherches de science religieuse* 54 (1966), pp. 417-25.

To update the article by M. Amann, "Malabres (Rites)," in *Dictionnaire de théologie catholique* IX (Paris, 1926), cols. 1704-45: there is no reworking of this article in the light of our new knowledge of the caste system, so one might profitably read the relevant chapters of *L'Histoire universelle des Missions catholiques,* under the direction of S. Delacroix (Paris, 1956ff.).

For developments at Rome before Vatican Council II, one must read the *Sylloge praecipuorum documentorum recentium Summorum Pontificum et S. Congregationis de Propaganda Fide* (Rome, 1939). The outlook is now completely outdated by what took place at Vatican Council II. Cardinal de Tournon's embassy is the subject of a massive study now under way by P. Francis A. Rouleau. The Gregorianum (in *Archivum Historiae Pontificae,* Vol. V) will soon publish a study of *Pope Benedict XIV and the Religions of East Asia,* from the time of the condemnations (1742 and 1744).

[2] E. Schillebeeckx, *L'Eglise du Christ et l'homme d'aujourd'hui selon Vatican II* (Le Puy: Paris, 1966), p. 22.

more real than ever before because of the shrinking world in which we live, makes the question of dialogue more urgent than ever before, and it also forces every religion to reflect upon itself.

It is worth noting here that the Council, in speaking of the Church of Christ, abandons the purely hierarchical point of view and is concerned primarily with the People of God which she leads. The stress has been shifted. The hierarchy itself disclaims any monopoly on churchliness, imbeds it instead within the heart of the Church, and attributes it first and foremost to the People of God to whom she renders service (*diaconia*).[3]

We have no intention of tracing this question in detail, of showing how this implicit view toward the apostolate in the world has always guided the activity of the great apostles and missionaries. Our intention here is to trace the major episodes in the dispute over the Chinese and Malabar rites which began around the time of the Renaissance.

I

THE AGE OF EXPLORATION

Living in an age of instantaneous communication, we find it hard to appreciate the profound effect of the "great discoveries" on European habits of thought. The man of the Middle Ages lived in a narrow world, shut off from outside influences. To be sure, he was aware of the existence of small enclaves of Jews who reminded him of the Old Testament world, but these people lived in ghettos that were almost hermetically sealed. When Islamism interposed itself between the Far East and the Mediterranean basin, the European's feeling of isolation was reinforced. Some travelers, of course, had managed to break through the barrier. Like Marco Polo, they made their way over a land route

[3] *Ibid.,* p. 46.

and returned by sea. Their astounding revelations about Cathay and Pango-Pango became legends and fired the European imagination.

Christopher Columbus took them more seriously, and thus discovered America for the Spaniards. The Portuguese, in search of Molucca spices, eventually rounded the tip of Africa. At Calicut they intercepted the commercial trade route which had previously been monopolized by the Muslims. Moving forward step by step, they reached Malacca (1511), Canton (1514) and finally Japan (1543). For several decades the Spaniards were wrapped up in the American venture, but Magellan's trip around the world in 1521 brought them in contact with their Portuguese rivals in the Pacific Ocean.

After interminable discussions between the cosmographers, which turned out to be fruitless because they were unable to determine the exact longitudes, a line of demarcation was finally agreed upon. It was a line with broad fluctuations, involving somewhere between 5 and 30 degrees of disputed territory. This eventually led to the creation of two episcopates in the "great Chinese archipelago", neither one too distant from the other: Macao for the Portuguese, in 1576, and Manila for the Spaniards, in 1581. The repercussions of this division on the Christian apostolate proved to be considerable.

Up to this point the average European had been able to cover his "home" territory with relative ease. He passed his life under the eye of God, who looked down upon him from close by, spoke to him, and sent him messages through his angels and priests. In this familiar world there was no room for startling surprises or disturbing doubts.

Gradually, however, the barriers surrounding him were being lowered and the horizon was stretching out before him. His outlook was being forcibly broadened, and a feeling of estrangement was setting in. He was made aware of principles of conduct that contradicted his own, of customs that differed radically from his, of beliefs that were opposed to those of his own faith.

The best example of the surprise involved is to be found in

Montaigne's *Essays*. In them the author tries to scrutinize everything methodically, to organize his life in terms of the many
strands of knowledge that were then coming to light. Montaigne
was an avid reader with insatiable curiosity. When he finally
came across the popular book of the Spanish Augustinian, Gon-
zalez de Mendoza, he eagerly read his story of the first missionary expeditions from the Philippines to the neighboring Asian
continent. Montaigne soon placed Chinese civilization at the
apex of the pyramid he had constructed to evaluate the recently
discovered cultures.

Montaigne was not the first European to be seized with curiosity about foreign cultures. The great humanist, Erasmus, had also
been deeply interested in them. In his letter to Paul Volz at the
time his *Enchiridion militis christiani* was reprinted (1518), he
opts for a peaceful conquest of the world instead of the traditional
crusade. He sees Christianity as something composed of con-
centric circles, the outer circles being less permeated with the influence of Christ. Christ himself is the immutable center that all
must try to draw near to: *Maneat Christus velut scopus*. In one
of his last books, *Ecclesiastes* (1535), he talks about the new
masses that would have to be Christianized and about the missionaries that would be required.

The case of the Franciscan priest Zumaragga, the first Bishop
of Mexico, should keep us from oversimplifying this matter and
making arbitrary classifications. While many of his contemporaries were being carried away by eschatological and apocalyptic
notions, he printed up a compendium of Christian doctrine and
topped it off by including excerpts from Erasmus' *Paraclesis*.
His evangelism, a product of radical Christian humanism, en-
listed the aid of Erasmus' *Enchiridion* to counter the vices of
colonial society in Mexico. He also printed up a new *Doctrina*,
which was in fact a plagiarized version of the *Suma* put out by
the Canon of Seville, Constantino Ponce de la Fuente, who was
later condemned by the Spanish Inquisition for Erasmianism. Another Franciscan, Bernard de Sahagun, was the first to devote
his life to a close and sympathetic study of Aztec civilization; his

writings were confiscated and were not rehabilitated until the 18th century. Around this same period a Jesuit priest, José de Acosta, drew up a scale which evaluated the various civilizations. He placed the "savage tribes" on the bottom, the Aztecs and Incas in the middle, and the Chinese at the top along with other Far East cultures that had benefited from Chinese civilization (the Japanese, for example).

Meanwhile, the Portuguese had established small colonies throughout the Indian Ocean, from India to Indonesia and beyond. They asked that Jesuits be sent to instruct the people who had been baptized by the vicar general of the Goa diocese. Francis Xavier, fresh from the University of Paris, was sent to do this work. In approaching the members of this lowly caste, he adopted simple missionary methods. It seems that he was not disturbed by the seemingly superstitious character of certain native customs, although the Portuguese "Europeanizers" looked on them with disdain. When he reached Japanese soil (August 15, 1549), he was confronted with a culture and a religion that was totally different from the Gospel he preached. His first experiences were very discouraging, and he soon realized that the "question of terms" was a very complicated one: in other words, he found that it was not easy to find the right Japanese words to use in preaching the Gospel. When he had returned to India and was preparing to set out for China, he decided it would be a good thing to make use of Constantino's *Suma,* which was also being used by Zumaragga in Mexico. But he did not broach the question of the religious value of Buddhism and Shintoism.

II

THE FAR EAST AND INDIA FROM 1552 TO 1693

Francis Xavier worked in the pre-Trent era (1545-1562). His spiritual heir in India and the Far East was Père Alexander Valignano, the Jesuit superior general of these regions from 1573 to 1606. Following in the footsteps of Xavier, he stimulated the advancement of Christianity in India, Malacca and Indonesia; he always insisted upon the necessity of knowing the language and local customs of the region, and he also helped to stimulate the progress of missionary work in feudal Japan. In the latter country he solidified relations with the local lords and, following the directives of the council, he molded missionary helpers native to the region. The arrival of four small Japanese "princes" in Rome, on an embassy to the Holy See, created a great stir in Europe (1582-1590).

China itself remained a closed country, even though the Portuguese had set themselves up in Macao, not far from Canton. Valignano realized that the Chinese mandarins' disdain for Europeans was based to a large extent on the fact that missionaries had been content to pick up only a cursory knowledge of various local dialects. He put a Sicilian, Michael Ruggieri, to work studying the written language (Mandarin Chinese) which was used at court and among the educated class. Following the Japanese style, Ruggieri adopted the dress of the Buddhist bonzes who professed Mahayana Buddhism ("the greater vehicle").

Matthieu Ricci was Ruggieri's successor, and had the approval of Valignano. He chose to sever ties with the native religions and to present himself as a European wise man who carried with him the pure Law. With the help of some neophytes, Paul Siu Kwang-ki among others, he made it to Peking, the capital city. There he died in 1610, "leaving the door open" for his successors. He had made a close study of the prevailing customs among the Confucianists, and he was convinced that "properly understood" they could be preserved in large part because they were "completely devoid of idolatry and even perhaps of superstition".

This approach was maintained by his successor in the China mission, Père Nicolas Longobardo, except on one important point: the terms to be used. In contrast with the exegesis of contemporary commentators on the classical texts, Ricci had rejected the materialistic interpretation and had argued for the spiritual outlook of the ancient Chinese. Some young missionaries to Japan, expelled to Macao in 1614, were impressed by the worship of Confucius in the latter region; they felt it was modeled on the cult of Buddha and other Shintoist divinities, and they spoke out against the terminology of Ricci. The Jesuits were divided into two factions, pro and con, and the debate was lively.

Père Longobardo wrote a piece opposing Ricci's position. It was eventually condemned to a bonfire, but fragments of it survived; it was later printed up in Europe, where it stimulated a courteous exchange between Malebranche and Leibnitz.

Meanwhile, Ricci's bold approach in China found an admirer in India: Robert de Nobili, another Italian. From the time the Portuguese had established themselves at Goa (1511), one question had persisted: Was the caste system essentially "religious" in nature, or was it simply a social phenomenon? On the whole, the various ecclesiastical synods concluded that in practice it was a superstitious practice, headed by the Brahmins who were akin to "priests". The "Europeanized" Christians adopted a completely different way of life.

De Nobili conceived a new approach while he was living in Madura (1606). He would dissociate himself from the lower castes, such as the Paravers, and from the priests who worked among them. Ricci's example encouraged him to take this step and to adopt an approach that might show that the customs of certain castes were purely social in nature. Some people belonging to the upper castes had renounced the world. These people were called "sannyasins", and they came from upper castes such as the Kshatriya. As sannyasins, they were allowed to associate with the Brahmins. De Nobili presented himself as a European sannyasin, and thus had to break contact with his European confreres because their customs (eating meat, drinking wine, etc.) and their contact with the untouchables were unacceptable. In return, however, he was initiated into the study of the Hindu texts, and he aroused the interest and curiosity of his new associates. He even managed to convert some Hindus belonging to the Nayakkar caste (a local one) and to the Brahmin caste itself.

On the Catholic side, however, he was accused of giving in to superstition and of betraying the true religion. His reply was that the caste system was merely an extreme form of social and class distinction, something which was quite common in Europe. He felt that he should not be any more strict than Christ's first apostles had been, because his purpose was to save souls, not to reform the social structure.

Pope Gregory XV eventually vindicated his approach on certain customs, if not on everything, in a Bull dated January 31, 1623. It is also worth noting that St. Robert Bellarmine, who had received a bad impression from the accounts he heard in Rome, later changed his negative attitude and opted for "tutiorism" (the "safer course").[4] Using this principle, he was able to give his approval to the commentaries of Matthieu Ricci, which were brought to Rome in 1616 and translated into Latin by Père Nicolas Trigault. Trigault also obtained an authorization in favor of the Chinese liturgy,[5] but it was never put into practice.

Trigault eventually returned to China, laden with gifts and books, only to find himself in the middle of the controversy over various rites. At this time there was still no central governing body charged with the supervision of missionary work; the Propaganda Fide Congregation was finally established in 1622. Before that date, Jesuit missionaries would submit their *casus conscientiae* to the professors of the Roman College.

After 1631 the whole situation was changed. When the Manchu dynasty conquered China (1644), police surveillance diminished. Missionaries were no longer forced to take a route through Macao and Canton. Thus two missionaries from the Philippines, the Franciscan Antonio de Sancta Maria and the Dominican Ange Cocchi left Formosa and landed in the maritime province of Fukien. There a strong traditionalism prevailed,

[4] *Auctarium Bellarminum,* p. 641: "Si rei certitudo non possit ad liquidum apparere, debet omnino operans tutiorem partem sequi, et nulla ratione, nullius imperio, nulla temporali utilitate proposita, ad minus tutam partem declinare."

[5] On the controversy over the Chinese liturgy, see F. Bontinck, *La lutte autour de la liturgie chinoise aux XVIIe et XVIIIe siècles.*

involving ritual ceremonies in honor of Confucius and the family dead. The two Philippine missionaries were shocked when they saw how the Jesuit converts were acting because they were used to the setup in Manila which put severe restrictions on the Chinese (New Year Feast forbidden, long hair banned, etc.).

When they began to study the Chinese characters, they came to realize the meaning of the sacrifices offered to Confucius and the ancestral dead. The Jesuits had borrowed this idea and used it to signify the sacrifice of the Mass. Disturbed by what they had learned, and by several other liturgical innovations, they applied to the authorities at Macao. The authorities, however, were not informed about what went on within China itself, and the military insurrection made it difficult for them to obtain exact information. The missionaries alerted the Philippine bishops, who then sent a letter of inquiry to Macao. The letter was answered by the old Jesuit provincial, Manuel Dias, but his reply did not satisfy them. The bishops decided to carry the matter to Rome, and the Dominican Juan Moralez was authorized to discuss the matter with the Holy Office and the Propaganda Fide Congregation.

The whole matter was handled in a very correct manner, and the Jesuits of China soon learned that Rome had condemned their course of action (September 12, 1645). They replied that they had only sanctioned these rites to the extent that certain modifications, which seemed called for by Christian orthodoxy, were added to them. Father Martini was entrusted with the task of presenting their case to Rome, and on May 23, 1656 a second reply came from the Roman congregations. It was the time when Propaganda Fide was preparing its first set of instructions to the vicars apostolic (published in 1659), which was later to become the Magna Charta of the missions (under Benedict XV in 1919): "Forbid nothing; proceed *sensim sine sensu,* so long as a thing is not clearly and unmistakably contrary to faith or morals."

Thus two replies had come from Rome, the one contradicting

the other. When this was pointed out to Rome, the Holy Office replied that both judgments were valid insofar as they were based on two different sets of facts (November 13, 1669). The missionaries in China were divided into two camps. The Jesuits in general, basing their position on probabilism, felt that these rites should be given the benefit of the doubt. Some of them, in fact, came to see parts of the classical Chinese texts as equivalents to the Old and New Testament.

The difficulties raised by Père Longobardo with regard to the proper terms were aggravated by the rites controversy. Bishop Maigrot, who succeeded Bishop Pallu as vicar apostolic, examined the texts thoroughly and issued a famous prohibition against their use (March 26, 1693). His decision was based on the way some commentators interpreted the classical texts.

A tragic event occurred in Tanjore, India while this controversy was raging, and it served to heighten the dispute going on in Rome. A Portuguese Jesuit, John de Britto, was put to death in cruel fashion. A beatification process was started immediately, but it ran into the same problems that had cropped up in connection with de Nobili. Although there were no more "sannyasin" priests like de Nobili, Britto had belonged to a class of missionaries known as "pandaram". Like the sannyasins, they too renounced the world, and they were accredited members of the Chutra caste. Ritually, there was complete separation between this caste and the Untouchables (Pariah); here, on another plane, was the problem that had been raised by de Nobili.

At first Rome had been inclined to approve accommodations to the social customs of the upper castes, so long as superstition and idolatry were ruled out. But it was particularly sensitive on the question of discrimination between Christians in the sanctuary itself. The problem was particularly acute at Pondicherry, where two Christian communities worshiped alongside each other in different buildings. Thus Rome was being pressed to take a clear stand on both the Chinese and the Malabar rites at the same time.

III

THE CONDEMNATIONS FROM ROME (18TH CENTURY)

The condemnations which were issued by Rome in the first half of the 18th century share a common characteristic. Not only superstition itself, but the very semblance of superstition, was vigorously proscribed. In 1700, under the persuasive influence of Bossuet, the Sorbonne took a stand against the *Nouveaux Mémoires concernant les Chinois* by Father Louis Le Comte (1696). This action does not seem to have influenced the discussions in Rome directly, except insofar as Bishop Maigrot's prohibition was brought into play. The prohibition against the Chinese rites was already drawn up, but not yet promulgated, when Pope Clement XI decided to send an embassy to the Manchu emperor Kang-hi.

The emperor had already been approached by the Jesuits in Peking and asked to issue a rather ambiguous decree which stressed the civil and political character of the rites in question. Adversaries of the Jesuit position reproached them for presenting a religious issue to a civil court. Moreover, one of the Jesuits, Father de Visdelou, who was well versed in the Chinese classics, expressed his disapproval of this course of action.

Cardinal de Tournon set out for the Far East without stopping in Portugal. While stopping over at Pondicherry, he condemned the Malabar rites (June 23, 1704). At Canton, Visdelou confirmed him in his unfavorable judgment of the Chinese rites; when his embassy to the emperor failed to come off, he published the interdict (Nanking, February 7, 1707). Visdelou, repudiated by his confreres, was named a bishop by de Tournon and he took up residence at Pondicherry. Thus he became the faithful correspondent of Propaganda Fide for both the Chinese and the Malabar rites.

The missionary situation in China worsened considerably. Reacting to the condemnation, the emperor Kang-hi demanded that every missionary sign a deposition that supported the position of Ricci. Two of the staunchest opponents of the Chinese rites—Bishop de Leonissa (an Italian Franciscan) and Bishop Maigrot (the author of the 1693 prohibition)—became convinced that the China mission would come to naught unless the promulgations of Clement XI (September 25, 1710, and March 19, 1715) were relaxed to some extent. Through private channels they asked for eight privileges or permissions.

A second pontifical ambassador was sent to Kang-hi. This ambassador, Cardinal Mezzabarba, was received and approved by the Portuguese king at Lisbon. But Mezzabarba did not fare any better at Peking. On November 4, 1721, at Macao, he granted the eight privileges requested by Leonissa and Maigrot, but it did not take long to realize that this step, for all practical purposes, nullified the original condemnations. The Chinese question was taken up with the utmost care once again, this time under the guiding hand of the Roman pontiffs themselves.

At about the same time the beatification process of John de Britto was introduced in Rome, at the insistence of the king of Portugal. During the proceedings held by the Sacred Congregation of Rites, the "devil's advocate" (and Visdelou) reminded those present of the earlier condemnations of the Malabar rites. Cardinal Lambertini, who was to become Benedict XIV, set this objection aside. When he became pope, he used all his knowledge of canon law to reach a decision on the question. It was no easy task.

Reading his top-secret correspondence with Cardinal de Tencin, we can trace the development of his thought week by week. He eventually fell back on the position that had been worked out, in general terms, by Robert Bellarmine: "Where the first commandment of God is concerned, tutiorism is the only acceptable course." Thus Benedict XIV once again promulgated the condemnations against the Chinese rites (July 11, 1742) and the Malabar rites (September 12, 1744). And he made the situation more difficult by requiring every missionary to swear a written oath (in triplicate), under pain of being recalled to

Europe. Moreover, he forbade the publication of any written material on the question which did not have official approval from the Propaganda Fide Congregation.

At this point it seemed that the door had been closed on possible accommodations to national rites. But one episode will show that Rome's position was a bit more subtle and involved than it might seem at first glance. Norbert, the Capuchin who had delivered a glowing eulogy at the funeral of Bishop de Visdelou (November 11, 1737), was foolhardy enough to seize on the papal condemnations as an excuse for proclaiming the deep-seated maliciousness of these rites. He called into question the beatification process of John de Britto. Pope Benedict XIV took it upon himself to get a condemnation of Norbert from the Holy Office; after a very stormy session, he himself put Norbert's *Memoires* on the Index (April 1, 1745).

This would indicate that these rites could indeed be "de-sacralized". However, every attempt to win some concession or relaxation from Rome met with the same fate. Thus, for example, when the emperor of Vietnam, Gia-Long, tried to satisfy Bishop Pigneau de Behaine by issuing a decree on the secular character of ancestral worship, he received this reply from Rome: "These things are not evil because they are prohibited; they are prohibited because they are evil." [6] Many Church historians (e.g., Rohrbacher and Brucker) were called to order when they took a different position. Only Pastor, in his *History of the Popes,* managed to get away with substituting "certainly not superstitious" for "probably not superstitious", the byword of the moderate advocates of the Chinese rites.

A contemporary practice, Haitian voodoo, is enough to show that the danger of perversion is not an idle threat. However, the condemnation of Norbert indicates that these rites were not condemned because they were intrinsically evil, but rather because they seemed evil in the eyes of public opinion. If public opinion were to change, the line of demarcation between religious and non-religious realities would shift. This is precisely what hap-

---

[6] *"Non mala quia prohibita, sed prohibita quia mala."*

pened in 1920 when Msgr. Batiffol and Louis Brehier shed new
light on the Shinto rites of Japan. Repeated statements of Japanese authorities showed that one had to make a distinction between two types of Shintoism: a religious Shintoism and a civil
Shintoism, the latter being perfectly acceptable.

Political turmoil in China has precluded the promulgation of
similar official statements in that country, but the attitude of the
ruling class has been clear enough to warrant a similar judgment.
In 1919 Pope Benedict XV reiterated the 1659 Instruction concerning national customs: "Sensim sine sensu, condemning only
those things that are patently contrary to faith or morals." The
papal constitutions of 1936 and 1939 repealed the earlier pro-
hibitions of Benedict XIV—first with regard to Manchuria (then
under Japanese control), then with regard to Japan itself, China,
the Far East countries (e.g., Vietnam) and India, and eventually
other mission territories such as the Congo. One might think
that that would be the end of the whole matter, but Vatican
Council II opened up a whole new perspective on the question.

IV

THE RELIGIOUS DIMENSION

Throughout the period of great explorations, when Christianity was spreading through new territories, a common attitude
prevailed. Even the most zealous partisans of the Chinese and
Malabar rites took great pains to show that these rites were of
secular origin, or else had ceased to be religious somewhere
along the way. Matthieu Ricci, for example, remained firmly
opposed to anything that smacked of Buddhism or Taoism. He
accepted Confucianism only because its educated representatives constituted a formal academy. Robert de Nobili, living in
Madura, posed as a European "sannyasin", a perfect European
counterpart of the men in the upper castes who had renounced
the world. In defending John de Britto from the attacks of
Norbert and his partisans, Pope Benedict XIV tried to maintain

the legitimacy of these "rites" to some extent—at least the way de Nobili practiced them.

A national religion is usually closely bound up with a nation's political and social structure. Therefore, this negative attitude toward the religious element was in effect a subversive approach. It sought to implant Christianity by wiping away the nation's past heritage. The disastrous consequences of this approach were spelled out superbly by the Vietnamese emperor Gia-Long in a friendly discussion with Bishop Pigneau de Behaine; the latter could not make one word in reply.[7]

Vatican Council II adopted a new approach. "Taking as its base the principle of religious freedom, the Council assumes that the religious dimension is one of the things that makes man what he is. . . . Nostra aetate finds that behind every religion there is a 'perception of that hidden power which is at work in the course of events and in human lives' (n. 2). The various existing religions are formalized expressions of that initial perception, molded by the native genius of a given people. . . . For the first time in her history, the Church has officially abandoned the monopoly on religious values which she had claimed for herself, even while she seeks to safeguard the unity of Christendom. Thus she adopts a new attitude toward non-Christian religions, and toward humanity as a whole in its quest for the deeper meaning of human life. . . ."[8]

The consequences of this fundamental doctrine are far-reaching, and they are carefully documented by the Council: "Man's religious sense, formally worked out in every religion, finds its authentic content only in Old Testament revelation and that of Christ himself, who founded his Church to continue his salvific work. This is the central message of the Council. The religious phenomenon finds its basic form in the Church of Christ. Ecclesial Christianity is the objective and full-blown expression of every true religion. Thus the Council provides us with the funda-

[7] See A. Launay, "Histoire de la Mission de Cochin-chine 1658-1823," in Documents historiques (III, 1771-1823) (Paris, 1925), pp. 225ff.
[8] E. Schillebeeckx, op. cit., pp. 41-43.

mental principles for a pastoral approach to present-day humanity. Present-day man may be religious or even Christian at heart, but he is on his way to becoming a non-practicing religionist." [9]

Seen in this perspective, the controversy over the Chinese and Malabar rites represents one stage in the formulation of a theology of revelation and its spread throughout the world. The vicissitudes of this effort would suggest that we should take a new look at the early days of Christianity and see how it carved out a path for itself among the religions of the Greco-Roman world.

[9] *Ibid.*, p. 45.

Georg Schwaiger / *Munich, W. Germany*

Catholicism and the Enlightenment

Anyone seriously interested in the Church and the world of today has to face the issues thrown up by the Enlightenment sooner or later. Whatever view one takes, it cannot be ignored in contemporary history. Modern man is inextricably involved in it. It started from England and the Low Countries, and its philosophical roots lie buried in the systems of Descartes, Francis Bacon and Baruch Spinoza. At the end of the 17th century it spread to France and Germany, and from there to the other countries of Europe, and lastly to those regions where European culture penetrated, such as New England and Spanish America. It really came into its own in the 18th century when it became the dominant outlook on life, particularly among the educated. It was this 18th-century Enlightenment which determined in large part the mentality of the 1900's when it provoked powerful reactions, as in idealistic philosophy, romanticism, the "restoration" movement or in various Evangelical and Catholic revivalist movements.

Much ink has been spilt on the debate about the rights and wrongs of the Enlightenment, and even today this debate still continues. The bitter controversies of earlier days, however, have now yielded to a calmer and more factual discussion. The way to a fair assessment of this Enlightenment, particularly from the Catholic point of view, was paved at the beginning of this cen-

tury by the Church historian Sebastian Merkle, of Würzburg
(1862-1945). In his sharp exchanges with Johann Baptist
Sägmüller, a canon law professor of Tübingen who was no less
emotionally involved, it became clear that distinctions had to be
made and that such a radical and revolutionary movement cannot just be condemned *in toto*. "Enlightenment", which meant
for some the promising start of a new age of freedom, of the
spirit, of civilization and humanity, and for others an abomina-
tion of destructiveness, came to be seen by Catholics, too, as a
very complex phenomenon in Western history. It was Merkle
who, from the beginning, showed the deeper understanding and
the better arguments.[1]

I

ENLIGHTENMENT AND CHRISTIANITY

The age of Enlightenment was the last to represent Western
culture as a whole, and as such it covered more ground geo-
graphically than any previous age. The "world culture" of today,
already accepted among scientists, is ultimately the consequence

[1] S. Merkle, *Die katholische Beurteilung des Aufklärungszeitalters*
(Berlin, 1909); *ibid.*, *Die kirchliche Aufklärung im katholischen Deutsch-
land* (Berlin, 1910). The first study, still a standard work today, is
included with other essays by the same author in Th. Freudenberger
(ed.), *Sebastian Merkle. Ausgewählte Reden und Aufsätze* (Würzburg,
1965). Of the abundant literature I mention only W. Philipp, *Das Werden
der Aufklärung in theologiegeschichtlicher Sicht* (Göttingen, 1957) and
F. Valjavec, *Geschichte der abendländischen Aufklärung* (Vienna/Mu-
nich, 1961). For the rest I refer to the bibliographies in recent general
works: A. Fliche and V. Martin, *Histoire de l'Eglise:* in Vol. 19, E.
Préclin and E. Jarry, "Les luttes politiques et doctrinales aux XVIIe et
XVIIIe siècles," 2 vols. (Paris, 1955-6); in Vol. 20, J. Leflon, "La crise
révolutionnaire, 1789-1846" (Paris, 1959); W. Anz, M. Greiner and W.
Maurer, "Aufklärung," in *Die Religion in Geschichte und Gegenwart* I
(Tübingen, ³1957), pp. 703-30; A. Schwarz, E. Hegel and L. Scheffczuk,
"Aufklärung," in *Lexikon für Theologie u. Kirche* I (Freiburg i. Br.,
²1957), pp. 1056-66; F. X. Seppelt and G. Schwaiger, "Das Papsttum im
Kampf mit Staatsabsolutismus und Aufklärung," in *Geschichte der
Päpste* V (Munich, ²1959); K. Bihlmeyer and H. Tüchle, *Kirchenge-
schichte* III (Paderborn, ¹⁷1961); F. Heyer, "Die katholische Kirche vom
Westfälischen Frieden bis zum Ersten Vatikanischen Konzil," in *Die
Kirche in ihrer Geschichte* IV, eds. K. D. Schmidt and E. Wolf (Göt-

of that Enlightenment of the 18th century. A fact of such importance cannot be ignored by the theologian, particularly when he realizes that this Enlightenment brought about a critical situation for Christianity as a revealed religion which, in the seriousness of its threat, can perhaps only be compared with the Gnosticism that surrounded the early Church.

Nearly all the questions that trouble our age were already broached in the 18th century. The Renaissance, humanism and the Reformation may have deeply affected the course of events in Europe, but they did no more than slacken the hold and validity of tradition; they did not break it. The decisive change came with the Enlightenment. How revolutionary this change was in every field may be seen when we compare the situation of the mid-18th century with that of the mid-19th. The process of disintegration is well known in history, when all kinds of tradition have accumulated and been found too burdensome. This process usually takes place under certain pressures. The Renaissance and the Reformation sought to free man from the "burden" of history. Both seized, for this purpose, on some original element within the framework of history: the Renaissance seized on the "ideal" man of pagan antiquity, while the Reformation turned to the "free Christian man" of "the pure Word of God" and "the unadulterated Gospel". But the Enlightenment, the most comprehensive and radical attempt to free man from his burden in modern times, went beyond history and took its stand directly on man as an intelligent being. And so "the mind instituted the process against history", which, according to Wilhelm Windelband, is the true significance of the Enlightenment.[2]

1. What Is Enlightenment?

A famous answer to this question was given by Immanuel Kant, who marked the climax and victory of the philosophical

---

tingen, 1963); L. J. Rogier, "Die Kirche im Zeitalter der Aufklärung, Revolution und Restauration," in *Geschichte der Kirche* IV, eds. L. J. Rogier, R. Aubert and M. D. Knowles (Einsiedeln, 1966), pp. 3-174, 420-37.

[2] Cf. G. Söhngen, *Die Einheit in der Theologie* (Munich, 1952), pp. 288-304.

Enlightenment in an essay published in the *Berliner Monats-schrift* (1784): "Enlightenment is the casting off of that tutelage of which man himself is guilty. This tutelage is his inability to use his own mind without the guidance of someone else. He is guilty of this tutelage when it is not caused by a lack of intelligence but by a lack of decision and of courage. . . . *Sapere aude* (Dare to know) is therefore the motto of the Enlightenment." Here Kant was thinking mainly of religious matters, because there this tutelage is at its most damning and dishonorable for an intelligent human being.

Elsewhere Kant described his age as the age of criticism (*Kritik*), because "criticism" had broken through with a force never known before. Man—in this view—fully conscious of his own value, applies the force of his intellect to everything, without any compromise or any regard for the consequences, whether it is a matter of experimental knowledge in this life (and here the new "scientific" method made enormous progress) or of a possible transcendental reality insofar as it can be known by man. A 1000-year-old image of the world thus vanished before the observing, experimenting, calculating and carefully assessing mind of man. The unexpected success of this process stimulated man's self-confidence, more so in the ordinary bourgeois society, which was still young, than among the academicians who remained rather conscious of the limits of their knowledge. With a sense of triumph and faith in progress, people believed they would soon lay bare the secrets and riddles of nature and with their intelligence dominate that world which had for so long been ignored or wrapped up in childish fantasies.

This intellectual age of the Enlightenment was concerned more than any other with putting into practice the newly acquired knowledge. And here it achieved much in political government, the administration of justice, and education, from the ordinary schools up to universities and academies. It is only with the rise of this Enlightenment that torture disappeared from judicial processes, and that at executions the condemned were no longer subjected to hours or even days of torment. Only since that time were witches no longer burned and people no longer executed or harshly oppressed because they held a different faith. The basic rights of man, as they were incorporated in the American Declaration of Independence of 1776 and in the French National Assembly of 1789, and as they are still understood and upheld today, were the fruit of the Enlightenment. In substance these "human rights" represented a document of Christian freedom, a noble witness to the Christian tradition of the West in a now mainly secular, revolutionary world.

2. *Enlightenment and Revelation*

Kant's definition formulated the principle of the Enlightenment as essentially asserting the complete autonomy of the human mind. One and a half centuries before Kant this human mind, detached from any revelation, had already been propounded by Herbert of Cherbury as the sole foundation of his "natural religion", and by Lord Shaftesbury of his "moral sense". Unfortunately, the deism which arose at the same time put Christianity on the same level as this "natural religion" which was essentially a noble ethical system which recognized a "supreme being". Thus it divested Christianity of its unalterable revealed character. The worship of God as a cult appeared unimportant and superfluous, like the sacraments and the rest of this cult. The originators of this theory were not, on the whole, aware of being anti-Christian, yet much damage was done to Christianity and the Church. They encouraged an attitude of merely nominal Christianity which was widespread in the 18th and 19th centuries, an attitude which was content with "noble humanity". Instead of a live religion which put man into immediate relationship with a personal God there was now frequently an ethic, art and science, often linked with a vague and pantheistic sentiment about the world at large. It should, however, be stated that these and other phenomena were not so much produced by the Enlightenment as they were the expression of a mentality which had already been "secularized".

3. *The Enlightenment in France and England*

This Enlightenment takes on a different shape in different countries, which makes it almost impossible to make uniform judgments about this period. In this pronounced individualistic age one has to look for such judgments in biographies and monographs. Yet, some clear differences come to the fore when we compare one country with another. For instance, in England and Germany the Enlightenment preserved in general a sense of proportion. Insofar as religion is concerned, these countries show that the Enlightenment was mainly interested in keeping faith and knowledge strictly apart since history had so frequently and unfortunately confused them. The case of Galileo is an obvious illustration. In Germany it was particularly the influence of the profoundly religious Leibnitz which ensured that characteristic moderation in the movement.

Things were different in France where, before the Revolution, people did not enjoy the political and social freedom which prevailed in England. In France the Enlightenment became increasingly an undermining force, destructive and revolutionary. There rationalism, of Latin origin, born of the Renaissance and completed by Descartes, had developed the mechanical outlook on the world and on life most fully. The pluralism of the feudal system had led to a unified and centralized State. In matters of justice the crudely visible aspect and multiplicity of the medieval ordinances had been superseded by the systematic clarity of Roman law. Classical art was dominated by the demands of unity and symmetry while the "rules" and the Alexandrine verse held an almost exclusive sway over literature. Mathematics and mechanics led to the triumph of the human mind, and the main principle of philosophy became the "metaphysical doubt". The whole concept of the structures of the world was rooted in the intellectual self-awareness of the individual. A similar development took place throughout the West but it was given a particular slant by the classical mind of the French, and this aspect became universal in the 18th century. The French contribution was the more important as during this time the whole of Europe fell under the spell of the French spirit, the French language and the French way of life.

In England Thomas Hobbes tried, under Charles I, to provide an explanation of the State. According to him, the State was based on a contract between the prince and his subjects. And so he came to justify "enlightened absolutism". At the time of the second "glorious" revolution which drove out the Stuarts, John Locke drew an opposite conclusion from this "contract" theory—namely, the right to terminate the contract and, by the same token, the right to start a revolution. In this way Locke justified the State in England after the events of 1688. Theory and experience were thus made to support each other. Locke's ideas about life and the State influenced the French, who were however more acutely aware of the problem of understanding and history.

These French thinkers were literary men who clung to their ideas without an opportunity of testing them in practice, with the result that theory prevailed over experience. Thus Montesquieu developed the theory of the division of power on the basis of what existed in England. Voltaire tried to set man free from the "superstitions" of the "dark ages". His prayer for the Church was "trample down abuses" (*écrasez l'infâme*). Like Diderot and d'Alembert he covered all the Christian had considered holy up till then with mockery and contempt. The Physiocrats applied the ideas of the Enlightenment to the whole field of economics. Finally, the Encyclopaedists, so named after their great *Encyclopédie ou Dictionnaire raisonné* (begun in 1750), applied throughout the conclusion that the mechanical explanation of the world, extended to the human organism, leads to the denial of the soul and the denial of God, while in politics the contract theory leads to the sovereignty of the people. Over against this rationalism Rousseau emphasized "nature", "feeling" and "soul". His *Contrat Social* dispensed with all the traditional forms of society and pleaded for the realization of the "general will" in the "original" communities through a brotherhood of all classes in a republic, and in a universal world citizenship. The

French, more than any other nation, suffered from the gap between thought and history. It is this peculiar historical situation, this meeting of their "classical mind" with the curious political and social conditions of the *Ancien Régime,* which gave birth to the French Revolution. It was a revolt against tradition, and with it began the tradition of revolts.[3]

II

THE ENLIGHTENMENT IN THE "CATHOLIC" COUNTRIES

If the French Enlightenment was, in large part, so hostile to the Church, the reason lies in the thoroughly un-Christian character of the Court of Versailles behind its ecclesiastical façade, the gruesome wars of religion which flared up again in the violent repression of the Huguenots under Louis XIV, the barbaric treatment meted out to the Jansenists and those suspected of Jansenism, and finally the bitter feuds between Jesuits and Jansenists. The controversies about grace showed no grace whatever. The perpetual squabbles among the theologians had alienated many a noble mind from the Church. In the Jansenist conflicts it was frequently the Christian elite who became the outcasts. And so in the 18th century the French Church lacked the great witnesses and defenders that could have matched the brilliant band of scoffers. Hatred of the Jesuits, who had taken part so passionately in the Jansenist controversies, grew constantly until the pope was forced to suppress the Order in 1773. In 1751 Benedict XIV, who clearly saw the dangers of the time and had no illusions about what was required, wrote to his disloyal friend, Cardinal Tencin, bemoaning the fact that the theologians were wasting their energy on shocking controversies about trivialities and didn't understand how dangerous the English ideas were for the Catholic countries.

An assessment, from a Catholic point of view, of the age of

[3] Cf. F. Schnabel, *Deutsche Geschichte im neunzehnten Jahrhundert:* Vol. I, "Die Grundlagen" (Freiburg i. Br., ⁴1948); Vol. II, "Die religiösen Kräfte" (Freiburg i. Br., ³1955).

Enlightenment in the countries of southern Europe is, even more than in the case of France, bedevilled by the fate of the Jesuits in the 18th century, and the judgment is often distorted. The suppression of the Jesuits by the State in France, Spain, Portugal, the kingdom of Naples and Sicily, in Parma, and lastly also in the Papal States, was often accompanied by undue harshness or even by brutality. Nevertheless, one should not overlook the positive reforms brought about in Spain under Carlos III (1759-1788) or in Portugal under the ministry of Pombal.

In the Holy Roman Empire the influence of the Enlightenment passed in the 18th century from the Protestant States to the Catholic ones in the south and west. This was reinforced by direct influences from France and the fact that the writings of the French free-thinkers were widely read in Germany. Yet, in Catholic Germany this movement became prominent about the middle of the century. In Germany one can rightly speak of a "Catholic Enlightenment". Only a very few theologians and churchmen—and rather uninfluential ones at that—became so radical as to break with the Church and her dogmas. Most German bishops and many theologians, both secular and regular, concerned themselves with necessary reforms, as did some of the princes. They tried to use what was sound in the Enlightenment for the spiritual and temporal welfare of man in both Church and State. These men did not always make enough allowance for the religious conservatism of the people and their zeal was often clumsy and rash, but one cannot doubt the profound seriousness and the personal sincerity of practically all those who represented the Catholic Enlightenment in Germany.

1. Maria Theresa and the Enlightenment

The main centers of these enlightened reforms in Catholic Germany were the lands ruled by the Empress Maria Theresa (1740-1780) and her son Joseph II (1765-1790; sole ruler after 1780), i.e., the four great archdioceses of Mainz, Cologne, Trier and Salzburg with their chapters, the Frankish dioceses of Würzburg and Bamberg, the electorate of Bavaria, the court of the Duke of Württemberg, and the dioceses of Passau, Augsburg, Constance and Münster in Westfalen. For the rest, the influence of the Enlightenment penetrated into every diocese and cathedral chapter and into most of the monasteries, particularly those that were prelacies.

In these Hapsburg territories the great reforms of Maria Theresa fulfilled an urgent need, and were on the whole beneficial for both Church and State. The intelligent and energetic empress was herself steeped in the profound baroque piety of south Germany, devoted to the Church and open to the needs of her time. The universities were reorganized in 1752 under the direction of the cultured personal physician to the empress, Gerhard van Swieten, a Dutch Jansenist, while during the years 1774-1776 Abbot Stephan Rautenstrauch of Braunau inaugurated a new phase by a thorough reform of the study of theology.

The most powerful stimulus for all this came from the Austrian Low Countries, and particularly from the University of Louvain. The influence of the celebrated canonist Zeger Bernhard van Espen spread through his disciples throughout the realm, the Church of the empire and particularly the Hapsburg territories. His system was strongly inspired by the Gallicanism of the French Church and by the emphasis on episcopal autonomy over against the papal claims which were considered exaggerated. But he granted above all a far-reaching influence in ecclesiastical matters to the prince or the State. Professors of constitutional law attributed this ecclesiastical authority of the State to the "natural order of the State" during this period. One should not take too negative a view of these reforms of Maria Theresa on the ground that the Jesuits were shorn of their influence and the empress did not resist the pressures of the Court of Burgundy more strongly in favor of the Order.[4]

Many nobles who were loyal to the Church, such as Gerbert, prince-abbot of St. Blasius, greeted the necessary spiritual renewal with joy. The new organization of theological study

---

[4] The sources are usefully brought together in F. Maasz, *Der Josephinismus. Quellen zu seiner Geschichte in Österreich*, 5 vols. (Vienna, 1951-61), but the warning given in the text applies here.

eliminated a Scholastic system that had become fossilized. The sources of Christian doctrine, particularly the Scriptures and the Fathers, were again given their due importance. Room was made for biblical and Oriental languages as auxiliary sciences; Church history, patrology and pastoral theology at this time became separate subjects in the formation of future priests.[5] It is true that the danger of priests becoming more and more the servants of the State was soon evident. Progress was made in the education of the people, particularly in catechetics and preaching. The principles of Josephinism were already formulated during the reign of Maria Theresa, though as yet without that extremism which would later lead to serious conflicts with popes and bishops.

The empress was particularly concerned with one aspect in her ecclesiastical ordinances. Worried about a persistent crypto-Protestantism, particularly in the mountainous regions, she tried to find the real causes, which she correctly discerned in the lack of religious care bestowed on the people living there. The parishes were far too widely stretched out and for many months of the year the roads were impassable for both priests and people. And so the people turned for their religious needs to services at home, in small groups, with Scripture readings and sermons of a "reformed" character. Plans to set up many new parishes and to improve pastoral care had already been worked out during her reign. This expensive project, which demanded many sufficiently endowed churches and presbyteries, was to be financed from the superfluous wealth of the monasteries. Rome's reaction was rather reserved. However, these plans to use the Church's wealth for the improvement of pastoral care were shelved when Frederick II of Prussia launched his war against Austria. The empress was not inclined to expose herself to the slanderous accusation that she used monastic property in order to pay for the war.[6] When her son Joseph began to rule alone, Josephinism became turbulent and ran into trouble, mainly because he lacked the discretion of his mother. Autocratically he suppressed some 600 monasteries

[5] S. Merkle, *Die katholische Beurteilung*, pp. 10-23.
[6] R. Reinhardt, "Zur Kirchenreform in Österreich unter Maria Theresia," in *Zeitschr. f. Kirchengeschichte* 77 (1966), pp. 105-19.

in his own territories. Basically, he did not simply confiscate Church property but rather used it for other purposes. In the same way he erected new dioceses, numerous parishes and other such territories, which was strictly against canon law but was nevertheless a great achievement from which the Austrian Church has benefited to this very day. He was personally a religious man and his intentions were pure and remained so, even when at the end of his life he saw the collapse of so many of his rash projects.[7]

2. *The Enlightenment and Secularization*

For the man of the Enlightenment the baroque vestments were too heavy and sumptuous. Instead of vast, illusory spaces he wanted something that he could oversee; instead of exuberant sentimentality he needed rational clarity and sobriety; instead of heavenly-earthly pomp he demanded help and usefulness for man's everyday life. One should not overlook in an assessment of the great Catholic baroque culture the fact that during this period the hierarchy frequently passed by the great social needs of the lower social strata, particularly in southern Europe and Latin America, although there was no lack of urgent warnings. On the other hand, the Catholic Enlightenment showed some definite social features and human concern. It was no longer a matter of pious almsgiving but of popular education and social improvement. It is against this background that one must see the many reforms brought about by the German bishops, closely linked with those of Maria Theresa.

Enlightenment and the insistent demands of an increasing secularization prompted the ecclesiastical princes to improve conditions in their territories and to provide their subjects with everything that was considered "progress" at that time. During the last period before the decline of the State Church it had many cultured and spiritual-minded noblemen in its cathedral chapters and among its bishops. Their mind is clearly reflected in the pastoral letters of that time, such as the pastoral letter of the prince-

[7] J. Wodka, *Kirche in Österreich* (Vienna, 1959), pp. 293-312.

archbishop of Vienna, Johann Joseph, Count of Trautson, in 1752,[8] the year of the reform of the Universities. The archbishop made explicit mention of the suitability of sermons about the veneration of saints and shrines. He criticized, however, the running in and out of churches in order to gain as many indulgences as possible; he warned against putting more trust in the veneration of a saint and his shrine than in Christ's redemption and against worrying more about the regulations of a confraternity than about keeping God's commandments. He blamed the preachers for speaking too often about the veneration of saints, pilgrimages, indulgences and confraternities and too seldom about the great truths of religion; they preached about saints and said nothing about God, the Most Holy; they preached the graces to be obtained at shrines and forgot about Christ, the source of all grace; they emphasized indulgences and confraternities and made no mention of what is necessary, namely, the commandments of God and his Church and the teaching and merits of Christ.

These guiding principles, which are indeed applicable at all times, can be found in practically all German pastoral letters of this time. Almost all the bishops of the empire published similar exhortations. Particularly famous was the pastoral letter of the prince-archbishop of Salzburg, the Imperial Count Jerome of Colloredo, in 1782. He was a typical ecclesiastical prince of the Catholic Enlightenment. Simple, modest and irreproachable in his own life, he began with extensive economy measures in his own secular administration in order to promote education and the general welfare of his subjects without running into higher taxation. Even the young Mozart became acquainted with the retrenchments introduced in the archiepiscopal court. Justice and administration were simplified in his territory by the introduction of trenchant reform measures that set an example to the rest of the empire.

[8] For what follows, see F. X. Haimerl, "Probleme der kirchlichen Aufklärung als Gegenwartsanliegen," in *Münchener Theologische Zeitschrift* 12 (1961), pp. 39-51.

The same approach marked the ecclesiastical reforms contained in the pastoral letter of 1782 of this able personal friend
of Joseph II. Colloredo went further than his Viennese col-
league, Trautson. His aim was to cut out the defects that had
crept into the outward forms of religious practice and so to
create a Christianity purified of all irrelevancies and super-
ficialities. Over against the exuberance of a baroque veneration
of saints, particularly of our Lady, he stressed the central significance of the Mass and of the sermon as the proclamation of
the Word of God. Abuses connected with indulgences were re-
buked. He did not encourage the many processions, pilgrimages
and confraternities because of the frequent disorders and the
disruption of regular pastoral care. He concurred with the re-
duction in the number of the too frequent Church festivals that
had been ordered by Popes Benedict XIV and Clement XIV.
Particularly those pilgrimages that lasted for several days gave
rise to unseemly disorders. The pastoral letter reproved those
people "who waste their time at the expense of their home, their
family, their employers and the common good, sleep at night in
promiscuous heaps on layers of straw or in corners, and then
assault the confessional instead of approaching it with contrition".
They deprive the confessor of his calm and peace of mind, then
assault the communion rails in the same rough fashion, elbow-
ing their way back from these rails, and finally have a lovely
time in the taverns.[9]

In this letter Colloredo gave a coherent summary of his reform
projects and then gave them the widest possible publicity. Both
clergy and secular officials had to draw attention to the pastoral
letter whenever suitable. It was most popular in Austria, Bavaria
and the whole of Germany, and was even translated into French
and Italian. At the same time strong measures were taken to
promote pastoral care and the practical application of the reforms. It soon became clear that large sections of the population
were mounting a powerful active and passive resistance. A mali-
cious proverb went around in Salzburg: "This objectionable

[9] S. Merkle, *Die katholische Beurteilung*, p. 93.

Colloredo has no Gloria and no Credo." However, these pastoral letters of the Enlightenment, which always combined the ecclesiastical with the secular needs, achieved only a doubtful success among the people.[10]

III

THE CATHOLIC ENLIGHTENMENT

The healthy forces of the Catholic Enlightenment opened the way again to the Bible, the Fathers, a living liturgy and a preaching of the faith in the spirit of the Scriptures. The insipid moralizing of a few isolated Catholic theologians and preachers should not make us overlook this decisive fact. An attempt was made to bring the Bible to the people and to explain the liturgical actions. And so there were already, toward the end of the 18th century, in both France and Germany, good popular missals, translations and explanations of the liturgical texts and actions. This spiritual approach led to the contemporary concern with German Church music, a German ritual, and in general with more consideration for the vernacular within the Church. Occasionally a parish priest would start to say Mass in German. Several bishops and theologians stressed religious tolerance. Many noble minds rejected the evils of religious polemics and steered directly toward a reunion of separated Christians which, frankly, went occasionally beyond the boundaries set by dogma.

This religious tolerance and the abandonment of compulsion in matters of faith were two of the finest achievements of the Enlightenment. It led to freedom of worship for Catholic minorities in Protestant territories and later to the organization of pastoral care and a hierarchy. There were repeated demands for the readmission of the laity to the chalice among Catholics, and in general the theological faculties of the German universities aimed at a renewal of theology on a scriptural basis. Dogmatic

[10] G. Schwaiger, *Die altbayerischen Bistümer Freising, Passau und Regensburg zwischen Säkularisation und Konkordat, 1803-1817* (Munich, 1959), pp. 1-37, 368-98.

theology turned again to the language of the Bible. Among the greatest achievements was the effort to purge moral theology of that sheer casuistry which had turned it into a mechanical teaching about sin rather than a teaching about virtue. Some theologians tried to build up a doctrine of Christian life on the basis of the Bible. One should never forget that it was usually outstanding bishops and priests who pursued these reforms, and that they were mainly concerned with the correct proclamation of the Christian message. Even if in practice they were not always very enlightened, they had the right intention.

In the light of Vatican Council II which took up so many of the aims of the Catholic Enlightenment, we should do justice to the so-called Episcopalians and Febronians of that period. Their concern with episcopal autonomy over against an exaggerated papalism was a legitimate one. We have no right to condemn it wholesale as "against the Church" as 19th-century apologetics used to do. In the future we shall only be able to call "episcopalian" in the negative sense those theologians who reject the papal primacy. But this was not the case with the German archbishops of the late 18th century nor afterward with the aristocratic Dalberg and Wessenberg.[11]

The renewal of theology, the renewal of pastoral care, adaptation to the Gospel, christocentric preaching, a sympathetic understanding of the world and its problems, the liturgical renewal, a pastoral care based on this liturgy and a stronger emphasis on the vernacular, the religious peace and union of the separated Churches—all these major concerns of the Catholic Enlightenment are also the major concerns of the present. One of the tragedies of Church history is that the promises embodied in that Catholic Enlightenment were prevented from coming to fruition. The 19th century saw the rise of a Church policy which damned any criticism of the restored Church, any suggestion of reforms adapted to the age, as pernicious "Enlightenment", as tending toward a "Febronian nationalistic Church" and there-

[11] G. Schwaiger, "Carl Theodor von Dalberg," in *Münchener Theologische Zeitschrift* 18 (1967).

fore as unorthodox and "liberal" and a betrayal of the papacy. Dalberg and Wessenberg, the great theologians of Tübingen in the last century,[12] were, like Sailer,[13] frequently the butt of such accusations. Particularly a figure like Johann Michael Sailer shows that this Catholic Enlightenment brought forth men who were confidently determined to overcome the crisis that beset the Church and the faith in their firm loyalty to the old unchanged faith and their open understanding of the Church's task in a new age.

[12] J. Geiselmann, *Die Katholische Tübinger Schule* (Freiburg i. Br., 1964); L. Scheffczyk, *Theologie in Aufbruch und Widerstreit. Die deutsche katholische Theologie im 19. Jahrhundert* (Bremen, 1965).

[13] Ph. Funk, *Von der Aufklärung zur Romantik* (Munich, 1925); H. Schiel, *Johann Michael Sailer*, 2 vols. (Regensburg, 1948-52).

Marie-Joseph Le Guillou, O.P. / *Boulogne-sur-Seine, France*

The Mennaisian Crisis *

The philosophy of the 18th century and the Revolution of 1789 had so shaken the Church in France that it felt the effects for the whole of the 19th century. The essential task of all priests, after the revolutionary tornado, was to reestablish in the dioceses and the parishes the conditions necessary for the practice of religion. They set themselves to work at this task with devotion and self-sacrifice. But all too often, through a nostalgia for the time when the Catholic religion was the State religion, they insisted on an exact reconstruction of the conditions that had existed fifty years earlier. They discussed the same old problems and they fought the same old enemies. It was as if time had stood still for half a century. "We had to work

* There has been a renewal of interest in Mennaisian studies, not only in France but in the whole of Europe. Of the books published since 1960, the following should be mentioned: J. Derré, *Lamennais, ses amis et le mouvement des idées à l'époque romantique 1824-34* (Paris, 1962); *idem, Metternich et Lamennais* (Paris, 1963); L. Le Guillou, *L'Evolution de la pensée religieuse de F. Lamennais* (Paris, 1966); *idem, Les Discussions critiques, journal de la crise mennaisienne* (Paris, 1967); R. Colapietra, *La Chiesa tra Lamennais e Metternich* (Morcelliana, 1963); G. Verucci, *F. Lamennais, dal cattolicismo autoritario al radicalismo democratico* (Naples, 1963); Mgr. Simon, *Rencontres mennaisiennes en Belgique* (Brussels, 1963); K. Jurgensen, *Lamennais und die Gestaltung des belgischen Staates. Der liberale Katholizismus in der Verfassungsbewegung des 19. Jahrhunderts* (Wiesbaden, 1963); W. Roe, *Lamennais and England: The Reception of Lamennais' Religious Ideas in the Nineteenth Century* (London, 1966).

fast," writes a historian of the time, the future rector of the Catholic University of Lille, Louis Baunard, "for we did not have much time and most of the priests had to engage in the fight before they had learned how to handle their weapons. Their studies were curtailed and barely adequate. All the philosophy the clergy had was contained in a Latin manual, the rudimentary "Philosophy of Lyons",[1] and all their theology was in Bailly's volumes,[2] a compendium inspired by Gallicanism, and for this reason later put on the Index. The two introductory treatises on religion and the Church concentrated on a refutation of the deism of Rousseau and the Protestantism of Jurieu. "This Jansenism, by its intricate subtleties, held us up for a whole year on the treatise on grace. Canon law was not taught, and Church history was only learned by the reading aloud in the refectory of Fleury, Père Longueval, Baron Henrion and Bérault-Bercastel. Holy Scripture was an extra, taught chiefly by the exegete Dom Calmet, an old man who was as learned as he was uncritical. All this armor was worn out, rusty and no longer serviceable." [3]

1. The Real Problems

This detailed description shows the real problems. For clearly the work of reconstructing the Church in France should not have absorbed the energies of the clergy to such an extent that they ignored the realities of the world about them and worked in complete unawareness of the intellectual ferment in France and Germany during the 18th and early 19th centuries. As Lamennais observed in 1808 in his *Reflections on the State of the Church in France* during the 18th century, it was necessary

[1] In the *Institutiones philosophicae, auctoritate D.D. Archepiscopi Lugdunensis ad usum scholarum suae diocesis editae*, 5 vols. (Lyon, 1783), attributed to the oratorian Valla, who also published a summary on Scholasticism in Cartesian dress.

[2] This is the *Theologia dogmatica et moralis* by Louis Bailly (1730-1808), which came out on the eve of the Revolution and was used in about forty seminaries (cf. Bellamy, *La theologie catholique au XIX siècle* (Paris, 1904), p. 25.

[3] M. Baunard, *Un siècle dans l'Eglise de France 1800-1900* (Paris, 1900), pp. 370-71. Baunard goes on to say that he does not want to accuse venerable, honest and zealous men but the times themselves.

for the Catholic Church "which never before has had to face such dangerous attacks" [4] to call to her defense qualified specialists, good exegetes, Oriental scholars—in short an educated clergy. This renewal was all the more vital because the progress of lay and religious studies was extremely rapid.

"For the last thirty years an enormous amount of work has been undertaken and carried out devotedly by scholars of all countries. It is time that Catholic theology reaped the harvest that has been prepared for it. India, Tibet, China —the whole of the East reveals its ancient traditions, which provide fresh support to the faith by their marvelous conformity with Christian traditions, whose universality and permanence, those two great characteristics of all that is divine, becomes plainer every day. The fortunate researches into Egyptian hieroglyphics, which enable us to fix the exact date of the zodiacs of Esne and Denara, have made the objections advanced against the chronology of Moses henceforth untenable. It is already possible to hope that some of the secrets of that ancient people's theology, which until now has been so obscure to us, may be discovered, and that we may be able to compare with the accounts of Jewish authors the history of the Pharaohs written on the banks of the Nile. The comparative study of the languages and origins of peoples brings us back continually to the primitive data recorded in Scripture. Even the physical sciences, particularly geology and physiology, constantly provide by their progress new weapons for the defenders of religion to combat anti-Mosaic hypotheses and materialism. But this is but little compared with the benefits that would result from the renewal of the moral sciences. The science of law, one could say, needs to be created from scratch. All that exist are Protestant and philosophical theories . . . which are contributing to perpetuate the disorders which we see about

[4] H. Lamennais, *Reflexions sur l'état de l'église en France* (Paris, 1825), p. 121.

us. A false metaphysic has been equally harmful and has pushed minds along various paths to skepticism. The Church, in scholarship alone, has a magnificent task to perform: it is up to her to make the chaos fruitful, and for the second time to separate the darkness from the light." [5]

This ambitious, superhuman program was adopted, with great success it seems, by all those in the Congregation of St. Peter who formed part of the teams of Malestroit and La Chenaie, and above all by Feli who in 1828, in spite of uncertain health, himself taught "English, Italian, Hebrew, philosophy and theology".[6]

2. *Training*

A former disciple of Lamennais, Charles Sainte-Foi, otherwise known as Eloi Jourdain, describes a day in a Mennaisian "seminary", which gives us an idea of the novelty of the training of these future "missionaries"—who were to specialize in different branches of knowledge and produce genuine Sanskrit, Arabic and Persian scholars in addition to several future bishops —to teach in seminaries and colleges, to preach and evangelize. He writes: "Every afternoon, the morning having been devoted exclusively to theology and philosophy, was spent on the study of literature and languages." The reading of newspapers was not forbidden but recommended. Each man "had to spend three-quarters of an hour a day on it and, as with all his other reading, take notes and make analyses".[7]

In the following lines we can feel the breadth and power that Lamennais wished to instill into the studies, including the study of theology: "We should not be afraid to admit that theology, so beautiful in itself, so attractive, so splendid, as it is taught today in the majority of seminaries is a petty and degenerate Scho-

[5] H. Lamennais, *Des Progrès de la Révolution et de la guerre contre l'église* (Paris, 1829), p. 278.

[6] Letter to the Count de Senfft, Dec. 21, 1828, in *Correspondance E. D. Forgues* I, p. 492.

[7] Ch. Sainte-Foi, *Souvenirs de jeunesse (1828-1835)* (Paris, 1911), pp. 97-125.

lasticism, which repels students by its dryness and does not give them any idea of religion as a whole or of its wonderful connections with everything that is of interest to man, with all objects of all thought. This was not how St. Thomas conceived of theology; in his immortal works he made it the center of all the learning of his time. Adopt his admirable method of coordination and generalization, and add to this the profound vision, the high contemplation, the warmth and the life that we find in the Fathers; then you will be rid of that boredom and weariness which stifles in young men destined for the priesthood any taste for study and even any talent for it." [8]

In a world in which everything had changed—institutions, customs, ideas—what would be the use of the most ardent zeal, without knowledge of the needs of the society in which it was to work? "It is necessary to learn differently and to learn more, differently in order to understand better, more in order not to be left behind by the pupils we have been given to teach. It is not because they know that the enemies of Christianity are strong but because they are ignorant of its natural defenders." [9]

To know the society of his times and its needs, to establish a Catholic theology which took everything into account and would insure unity of belief among all men—this was Lamennais' constant endeavor. This was the purpose of the Juilly conferences of 1831 which resulted in the system of Catholic philosophy, and it was also the basis of the "preaching" of the journal *L'Avenir* whose famous slogan was "God and Freedom": "We firmly believe that the development of modern scholarship will one day lead not only France but the whole of Europe back to the unity of the Catholic faith, which will then later gradually draw to itself the rest of the human race, and establish it through the one faith as one spiritual society, *et fiet unum ovile et unus pastor.*" [10] But we cannot fail to be surprised that Lamennais continues as if this followed self-evidently: "But we believe also that today

[8] H. Lamennais, *Des progrès de la Révolution* . . . , *op. cit.,* p. 276.
[9] *Ibid.,* p. 277.
[10] Article of Oct. 18, 1830, by Lamennais, in *L'Avenir,* "De la séparation de l'église et de l'état," *Mélanges catholiques* I, p. 146.

religion should be completely separated from the State and the priest from politics; that Catholicism, which faces the opposition of nations and often the persecution of governments, would only be weakened the more if it did not hasten to shake off the yoke of their heavy protection; that it can only revive in freedom." [11]

Why did Lamennais insist so strongly upon freedom for the Catholic religion? Why did he so forcibly demand freedom of conscience, of the press, of instruction, of assembly, which brought upon him the public censure of the Roman curia, for whom these freedoms were "irreconcilable with the teaching and the practice of the Catholic Church", as R. P. Rozaven declared in a statement to support the condemnation of Lamennais? It was always for the same reason: the desire to make the Church more true, more in accord with the gospels and more relevant to the society of her day. He thought this would only be possible if priests, while being subject to the laws of their country like other citizens, obtained their freedom in the spiritual order by the total separation of Church and State. Lamennais, who was very conscious of the difficulties involved, proclaimed, in a manner that some would find exaggerated, that this separation was necessary because it was the only way that religion could be set free from the civil power and not be administered like customs and taxes. In this way the priest would no longer be the equivalent of a civil servant and thus subject to possible pressure from the government; in this way bishops would no longer be nominated by the civil power but by Catholics themselves, who would find a legal means of corresponding with the wishes of their head, the Holy Father.

3. *Freedom and Poverty*

Granted the separation of Church and State, the other freedoms demanded followed as logical consequences: freedom of instruction because it is the freedom of the family and without it true religious freedom or freedom of thought could not exist;

[11] *Ibid.*

freedom of the press because one must have faith in the truth and its eternal force rather than trusting in the rigors of the censor, "which never stamped out an error and which often lost the power to do so by lulling itself into a state of idiotic overconfidence and false security".[12] Finally, at a time when, according to Lamennais, governments should follow public opinion, it is necessary "that this public opinion should have, besides the government, a means of being formed and manifested in a way which cannot be despised or ignored".[13]

To one who would object to Lamennais that his ideas are revolutionary because they threaten to break the monopoly of the university and to create what we should call a trade union, and that furthermore with the suppression of the clerical budget they put priests and bishops in a desperate situation financially, making them literally beggars, he calmly replies: "Give me a hut for a presbytery, take a stone from the fields for your altar, and let the barn where you store your corn be your church. Do you think God would not prefer to be free with us under a thatched roof than enslaved with his children in a palace? Do you think that the priest in his hut will have neither mother nor sister and that his rough homespun will be less independent than silk?" [14]

The proof to Lamennais that what was possible for the early Church was still possible in his day was the example of Ireland, upon which Montalembert gave three stirring reports on the 1st, 5th and 18th of January, 1831, establishing that in this grievously poor country the Catholic religion was solidly supported financially, by each according to his means. What was true of Ireland and the Irish clergy could be true of France, and if there were districts where a dying faith offered few resources, this was, Lamennais insisted, because "this weakening of faith is due in part, though it grieves us to say it, to the lack of zeal and the lack of a true priestly spirit among the pastors. Whenever they

---

[12] Article of Dec. 7, 1830, "Des doctrines de l'Avenir," *Mélanges catholiques* I, p. 14.

[13] *Ibid.*, p. 15.

[14] Article in *L'Avenir*, Feb. 2, 1830, "De la suppression du budget du clergé", *Mélanges catholiques* I, p. 209.

are what they should be, they will not lack what they need".[15]

This combination of freedom and poverty is absolutely essential for Lamennais. It is by suffering, physical wretchedness and poverty freely undertaken that one can feel solidarity with the whole of humanity and especially the oppressed and the poor and the weak who are tortured like Christ on the cross. The ministry of the priest should be especially to them: "They will be the priest's family, his beloved children, gathered, and cherished in his paternal heart, because by reason of their very sufferings and their tears, the only heritage that they receive or pass on, they are visibly Christ's privileged friends, because he too suffered poverty and pain and he said 'Blessed are those who weep.' " [16]

4. *Theological Crisis*

This brings out clearly the reasons for the crisis. The Mennaisian institutions, often works of genius, undeniably bore a prophetic character. His contemporaries were impressed by this call to return to the spirit of the Gospel and by the extraordinary aura of this little man who raged, all alone, poor and exhausted, against the mighty, the kings and the rich. But if many bishops were profoundly disturbed by his preaching, they were also men whose dignity and self-respect suffered from the violent denunciations of a simple priest whose qualifications for the job they might well question.

Lamennais was obsessed by the urgency of the message he had to deliver and he bothered very little about tailoring it to the concrete reality of existing institutions. He "charged", head down, taking no one into account, and often happily commingled as objects of his fury the incidental and the essential, the spiritual and the temporal. If ever there was a man to ignore diplomatic maneuvers, political cunning and half measures, it was Lamennais; for him it was all or nothing. Thus when he openly supported the Belgians and the Irish in their struggle to gain their

[15] *Mélanges catholiques* I, article of Oct. 18, 1830, p. 151.
[16] *Ibid.*, p. 85.

freedom, he was merely acting according to his principles. But he did not take into account that when, in his famous Act of Union of November 15, 1831, he summoned the liberal Catholics of France, Belgium, Ireland, Poland and Germany to join in one huge federation, he was ostensibly heading a movement which was more political than religious, and that people would regard him as a revolutionary, a visionary, a dangerous agitator, and no longer as a prophet. There were many in Rome who were prepared to forgive him his hostility to the Gallican French bishops because of the valuable services he had rendered to the Holy See; there were many clergy in France who were prepared to tolerate his doctrine of common sense and his Ultramontanism; but neither the Romans nor the French could stand for his liberalism which in their eyes was synonymous with agitation, civil strife and revolution.

Lamennais was angry and spoke of being betrayed by the hierarchy, and of their shameful alliance with the mighty of the earth, kings and emperors, against the people. It is certain for example, that the brutal repression of the revolt of Catholic Poland in 1831 against its Russian masters, and the indirect support given to Nicholas I, the schismatic Emperor of Russia, by Gregory XVI in his letter of July 9, 1832 to the bishops of Poland, in which he denounced the rebels who had plunged their country into suffering and recommended obedience to the legitimate government, did much more to precipitate Lamennais' religious crisis than the encyclicals *Mirari vos* and *Singulari nos,* whose own part was nevertheless so important.[17] Lamennais could no longer be in any doubt. Gregory XVI had allied himself with Nicholas I and betrayed his mission by approving and sanctioning brute force; thus he was no longer truly pope of the holy Church of Christ. What he did not know of—but how could he have known?—were the tears and the horror of this same Gregory XVI in the presence of the patriarch of Jerusalem when he was informed, a little late it is true, of the persecution of the

---

[17] On this subject cf. L. Le Guillou, *Les discussions critiques. Journal de la crise mennaisienne* (Paris, 1967), Ch. 2, "La crise polonaise."

Poles, which until then had been carefully concealed from him.[18] For Lamennais, who had an exaggerated tendency to divide the world sharply into good and evil, Gregory XVI could only be an evil man, a bad pope, the sinister ally of Nicholas I, and thus of Satan because he supported the strong against the weak and despised the holy laws of justice and humanity; and it was not only Gregory XVI whom he condemned, but the whole papacy, the whole Church, Catholicism itself. During the winters of 1833 and 1834 he came to think that the hierarchy was "divorced from Christ, the Savior of the human race, in order to fornicate with all his torturers".[19]

Lamennais' religious crisis was triggered by the "murder" of Poland and the hierarchy's position on freedom (1830-1). It led him at first into a tragic isolation, and then, through his fidelity to his conception of freedom and his conscience, to a tragic rupture with Catholicism.

The Mennaisian crisis is first and foremost a theological crisis concerning the relation between the Church and the world when man was no longer looked up as belonging to an authoritarian society in pyramid form. It was a crisis which could only be resolved by a deepened theological understanding, and this was not forthcoming.[20]

[18] Cf. A. Simon, *Rencontres mennaisiennes en Belgique*, Appendix, p. 259.

[19] L. Le Guillou, *op. cit.*, Fragment 3.

[20] L. Le Guillou and his brother, Rev. M.-J. Le Guillou, are bringing out three volumes of unpublished papers (Dominican and Jesuit letters, etc.) on the theological aspect of the Mennaisian crisis. M.-J. Le Guillou is bringing out a theological study based on these papers, *Les étapes de la crise mennaisienne.*

Thomas McAvoy, C. S. C./*Notre Dame, Indiana*

Americanism: The Myth and the Reality

The unity[1] achieved by the American hierarchy of the Roman Catholic Church in the Third Plenary Council of Baltimore was in one sense very deep and in another very superficial.[2] There was, to the amazement of American non-Catholics, a remarkable unity in essential doctrine and practice with, at the same time, a notable divergence in the personalities, the national origins and the education of the American hierarchy. The Council itself had been more or less imposed from Rome, although sought by some members of the American hierarchy. The legislation of the Third Plenary Council did not have for its purpose the solution of the peculiar problems of Catholicism in the United States but the reorganization of the hierarchy and the hierarchical institutions in the manner best suited to the purpose of the universal Church.

1. The Natural Divisions of American Catholicism

The membership of the Council was symbolic of the natural divisions of American Catholicism. Including Cardinal John McCloskey who was unable to attend the Council, and the

---

[1] I have treated the subject of Americanism in great detail in my book, *The Great Crisis in American Catholic History, 1895-1900* (New York, 1957).

[2] The official record of the Council is *Acta et decreta Concilii Plenarii Baltimorensis Tertii* (Baltimore, 1886).

apostolic delegate, Archbishop James Gibbons of Baltimore, the archbishops represented quite well the diverse elements of the hierarchy. Archbishop Elder with Bishop John Spalding represented the original Anglo-American origins of American Catholicism, but archbishops of Irish birth or descent were predominant. There were representatives of French, Spanish, German and Belgian immigrants. The national origins of the bishops showed an even more pronounced Irish predominance and had a better German representation, but had fewer prelates of other nationalities. Those of Irish birth or descent held the more important sees, especially those on the eastern seaboard.

Because most Irishmen spoke the English language from birth, because the American Irish did not think of themselves as foreigners, and because these Irish bishops held the chief sees, they tended to speak for Catholicism in the nation. This had two disquieting effects. As long as the Irish were the spokesmen for the Church in the country, Roman Catholicism was to be regarded by Americans as a foreign religion and that fact in turn was not pleasing to those of English descent and to those of other nationalities, especially to the German Catholics who had become very numerous in the dioceses of the near Middle West. In a sense the Third Plenary Council, by settling for the immediate future the Romanization of American Catholic canonical organization and practice, cleared the way for the discussion that followed on how much Americanization would be accepted and who should have the final word in that decision. Across this discussion ran the controversy that seems to exist in the Church at all times, the division between the progressives and the conservatives in the adaptation of the Church to the times. Sometimes these divisions seemed to follow nationalistic lines, sometimes not. Sometimes also the progress of Americanization of the Church seemed to arouse conservative fears, although at other times the conservatives seemed to be stronger American nationalists.

At the conclusion of the Third Plenary Council the nationalizing tendency seemed to be in the ascendancy, especially since the whole American Church seemed to be bound into the new unity by the regulations of the Council. It seemed quite appropriate that the presiding officer of the Council, Archbishop Gibbons, should be made a cardinal, especially since the first American cardinal, John McCloskey, had died on October 10, 1885. It seemed also appropriate that the first notable fruit of the Council should be the establishment of the first national institution of American Catholicism, Catholic University. There was no great difficulty in obtaining approval of the decrees of the Council since they had been for the most part prearranged by the meeting of the archbishops and bishops in Rome in 1883.

The exact character of Catholic University was not determined in the Council. There was also one other problem postponed for final settlement after the Council, that of the condemnation of certain secret societies which were attracting Catholics to membership in the United States. The question of creating a system of Catholic parochial schools seemed definitely decided, and the relationship between religious orders and the hierarchy was solved by adopting the solution obtained by Cardinal Manning in England. But no solution was offered for the problem of friction between the many nationalities composing the Catholic body in the United States.

2. *Americanization*

Whatever friction there had been in earlier times between the Anglo-American Catholics and the Irish immigrants was not caused by great differences in language between them because Gaelic did not survive even among the Irish who spoke Gaelic before they came. But the Germans, particularly in the Middle West, brought with them not only the German language, but frequently German sisters and brothers and, more importantly, German priests who tried in some measure to re-create the German Catholic communities that they had left behind in Europe. To the Irish particularly the perpetuation of these foreign languages and customs seemed undesirable and a hindrance to the advance of Catholicism in the United States. The German

Catholics who regarded the Irish lightly not only resented this criticism of the Irish and other Americans, but retorted with charges that American culture was permeated with religious liberalism and materialism manifested in easy divorces and ir-religion.

The first notable action of the Germans against Americaniza-tion was a petition in 1883 of 82 priests of St. Louis to Rome asking that their national parishes be given full parish rights. The Roman authorities referred the matter back to the Plenary Council, but no action on it was taken there.

When in 1886 Father P. M. Abbelen of Milwaukee presented a petition to the Sacred Congregation asking for full parochial status for the German national churches and that children of the immigrants be sent to these parishes, the American bishops in Rome—John J. Keane of Richmond and John Ireland of St. Paul —objected and the Council of archbishops meeting in Phila-delphia sent a protest against the Abbelen petition. The Sacred Congregation of Propaganda rejected the Abbelen petition on June 7, 1887.[3]

When Archbishop Gibbons, named cardinal on June 7, 1886, went to Rome early in 1887 to complete the ceremonies of his investiture, he was called into conference by the cardinals who were weighing a request by Cardinal Alexandre Taschereau of Quebec that the Knights of Labor be condemned as a secret society. Gibbons pleaded successfully against the condemnation. In some manner, his letter to the Congregation was published in the *New York Herald,* and because the condemnation of the Knights was prevented, Gibbons and Bishops Ireland[4] and Keane[5] who had assisted him achieved a reputation as friends of the American workingman.[6]

[3] The most sympathetic study of German Catholic immigration is C. Barry, O.S.B., *The Catholic Church and German Americans* (Mil-waukee, 1953). Abbelen is treated pp. 62-75.

[4] J. Moynihan's *The Life of Archbishop John Ireland* (New York, 1953) is an imperfect but friendly study.

[5] P. Ahern's *The Life of John J. Keane, Educator and Archbishop 1839-1918* (New York, 1935) is the best study of this archbishop.

[6] Cf. H. Browne, *The Catholic Church and the Knights of Labor* (Washington, 1949), especially pp. 228-312.

Bishop Ireland also emerged as a leading protagonist for Catholic University.[7] Then, as a leader in efforts to make Catholics accepted by Americans, he also drew upon himself the criticism of the German bishops of Wisconsin. The points of controversy between the progressive members of the hierarchy and the more conservative bishops were civic Americanization, the erection and maintenance of parochial schools, and cooperation with non-Catholics in social reform. In all three, Bishop Ireland became the chief exponent of the progressive or liberal side. In his speech at the Third Plenary Council he had said: "Republic of America. . . . Thou bearest in thy hands the hopes of the human race. Thy mission from God is to show to nations that men are capable of the highest civil and political liberty. Be thou ever free and prosperous. Through thee may liberty triumph over the earth from the rising to the setting sun!—*Esto Perpetua.*"[8] At Gibbons' golden jubilee he had exclaimed: "I preach the most glorious crusade. Church and Age! Unite them in the name of humanity, in the name of God!"[9] A few moments later, he said: "It is the age of democracy. It is an age of liberty, civil and political—the people, tired of the unrestricted sway of sovereigns, have themselves become sovereigns and exercise with more or less directness the power which was primarily theirs by divine ordinance. The age of democracy!"[10]

In his efforts to Americanize the Church, Bishop Ireland had close associates in Cardinal Gibbons and Bishop John J. Keane in this country and an ally in Father Denis O'Connell in Rome. Opposed to him were Archbishop Michael Corrigan of New York, Bishop Bernard McQuaid of Rochester and several German bishops. In 1890, addressing the National Educational Association in its annual meeting held in St. Paul, Ireland, now an archbishop, praised the public school system.[11] Then, under his

---

[7] D. Reilly, O.C., in *The School Controversy* (*1890-1893*), is partisan toward Archbishop Ireland in the school controversy: 2 vol. (New York, 1903-4).

[8] J. Ireland, *The Church and Modern Society:* I, pp. 64-65.

[9] *Ibid.,* p. 115.

[10] *Ibid.,* pp. 116-17.

[11] *Ibid.,* pp. 217-32.

direction, the pastors of parochial schools in his diocese at Faribault and Stillwater in 1891 made agreements with public school
authorities to turn over their parochial schools during the day
and in turn received public funds for the pay of teachers. Archbishop Ireland was subject to new criticism and charged with betraying the Catholic parochial schools even though the contracts
were soon cancelled. At the Council of archbishops in St. Louis
in November, 1891, Archbishop Ireland explained his action and
Cardinal Gibbons sent to Rome a report of the session that was
friendly to Archbishop Ireland. But Archbishop Corrigan of New
York, with the signatures also of other archbishops, sent in a
criticism of Archbishop Ireland's explanation. Archbishop Ireland went to Rome and the Sacred Congregation of Propaganda
ruled that his contracts in the Faribault and Stillwater schools
"tolerari potest".

3. Americanism

On his way back to the United States in 1892, Archbishop
Ireland spoke in Paris under the auspices of those who were
supporting the *ralliement* to the Third Republic, praising the cooperation between the Church and democratic institutions in the
United States.[12] In a second speech to the younger clergy of
Paris, he urged them to get out of their sacristies and work with
the people. In 1894, Abbé Félix Klein of the Institut Catholique
translated several of the archbishop's American speeches into
French and published them as a book.[13]

(a) *The Reality*. Certain documents and maps dealing with
Columbus were sought from the Vatican Library for the World's
Fair in Chicago. Pope Leo XIII agreed and decided also to send
a papal legate with the documents. The legate chosen was Archbishop Francesco Satolli who had defended Archbishop Ireland
in the controversy over the schools. The legate came under the
guidance of Monsignor Denis O'Connell and after attending the

[12] For Archbishop Ireland's visit to France, cf. McAvoy, *op. cit.*, pp.
100-107.

[13] J. Ireland and Abbé Klein, eds., *L'Eglise et le Siècle* (Paris, 1894).

opening ceremonies of the Chicago Exposition went for a visit with Archbishop Ireland in St. Paul. He went also to the annual Council of the archbishops in New York on November 16, and presented two proposals: a fourteen-point program for schools which seemed to approve what Archbishop Ireland had done in his archdiocese, and a proposal that there be an apostolic delegation established in Washington for the United States. The archbishops rejected both proposals. On the Satolli proposal for the schools there were so many bishops who wrote protests to Pope Leo that the pope sent a letter the following May insisting that Satolli had been misunderstood and that the decrees of the Third Plenary Council on schools were still in force. On the proposal about the delegation, while Cardinal Gibbons in the name of the hierarchy was preparing a letter rejecting the proposal, Archbishop Satolli released a letter of the pope on January 14, 1893, establishing the apostolic delegation with himself as first delegate.[14]

The delegate had taken up his residence at Catholic University where he was the guest of Bishop John J. Keane, a close friend of Ireland. Further, Archbishop Corrigan had refused to have anything to do with the delegate and was accused of fostering certain attacks on the delegate appearing in the press. Cardinal Gibbons, at the suggestion of Cardinal Rampolla, intervened and brought about a friendly meeting between the apostolic delegate and Archbishop Corrigan in New York in the summer of 1893. Yet, the delegate attended the Catholic Columbian Exhibition in Chicago in September in the company of Archbishop Ireland and gave high praise in his speech to the American Constitution.[15] The delegate refused, however, to have anything to do with the Catholic participation in the Parliament of Religions held about the same time at the World's Fair. Bishop Keane was the chief Catholic representative in the Parliament although

---

[14] The story of the apostolic delegation is told in J. Ellis' *The Life of James Cardinal Gibbons, Archbishop of Baltimore 1834-1921*: 2 vols. (Milwaukee, 1954), I, pp. 595-652.

[15] *Loyalty to Church and State, The Mind of His Eminence, Francis Cardinal Satolli* (Baltimore, 1895), p. 150.

several other Catholics, including Cardinal Gibbons, were on the program. Keane later wrote letters and newspaper articles in defense of his participation in the Parliament, but some other Catholic writers were very critical of the Catholic participation.

On June 20, 1894, the Sacred Congregation of the Holy Office issued a new decree banning Catholic membership in secret societies, mentioning especially the Odd Fellows, the Sons of Temperance and the Knights of Pythias. The conservatives, especially Bishops McQuaid of Rochester and Silas Chatard of Indianapolis and the German bishops of Milwaukee, wanted the condemnation, but Cardinal Gibbons, Archbishop Ireland and their friends asked the delegate not to announce the new decree and wrote to Rome to have it suspended. The Council of archbishops meeting in Philadelphia in October decided not to issue the decree, but some bishops had already announced it. Then, Cardinal Rampolla, on November 24, sent Cardinal Gibbons word that the decree should be published. That summer also, Father William Tappert from Kentucky had attacked the Catholic participation in the Parliament of Religions in a public Catholic meeting in Cologne. At the Third International Catholic Scientific Congress in Brussels in September, Keane had defended his participation and that of other Catholics, claiming that it had been an occasion of good. In Paris there arose a movement to hold a similar parliament in connection with the Paris World's Fair in 1900, but the plans were so liberal that the Cardinal-Archbishop of Paris disapproved the plan.

In May, 1895, Monsignor Denis O'Connell was forced to resign from the rectorship of North American College, apparently because of his partisanship for the liberal bishops. Cardinal Gibbons made him rector of his titular church so that he could stay in Rome and be of service there. On April 25, 1895, Archbishop Satolli attended the laying of the cornerstone of a church in a German congregation in Pottsville, Pennsylvania, and gave strong praise to the German Catholics of the country. This was a change of position on his part. Then, on August 12, he asked the pope for a letter condemning parliaments of religion. The papal letter was dated September 15. It caught Archbishop Ireland by surprise and at first he denied that it had any importance in American activities. It did kill the movement for a parliament at the Paris Exposition of 1900. In Rome in the *Civiltà Cattolica,*[16] a chronicle of events in the United States said that the liberals had received two checks, the condemnation of secret societies and the prohibition of parliaments of religion. The article accused the Americanizers of a kind of Pelagianism and of separatism.

On January 5, 1896, Archbishop Satolli was named to be a cardinal. In September, 1896, Bishop John J. Keane was removed from the rectorship of Catholic University. In the *Ecclesiastical Review* of February, 1897, there appeared an article, "The Chapter 'De Fide Catholica' in the Third Plenary Council of Baltimore," accusing the progressives of liberalism. On March 28, Ireland answered his critics from the pulpit of St. Patrick's Church in Washington, calling his opponents "refractaires" and accused them of being opposed to the ideas of Pope Leo XIII. He insisted that the divisions in the American Church were not over nationalities, but were over fidelity to the pope's wishes.[17] Monsignor Joseph Schroeder of Catholic University answered him in the German Catholic paper of Pittsburgh, accusing the progressives of the condemned liberalism of the Syllabus of Errors. The story of the dismissal of Keane had been told in Paris in *La Verité* by a friend of Schroeder, Abbé Georges Périès, a discharged professor of canon law from Catholic University, who repeated rumors that Ireland was to be called to Rome. Cardinal Rampolla eventually was forced to issue a denial of the story.

In the spring of 1897, Count Guillaume de Chabrol, an active leader in the *ralliement* movement in France, decided to publish a translation of the biography of Father Isaac Hecker (1819-1888), the convert founder of the Congregation of St. Paul. Chabrol saw the biography as a usable tool in his campaign for

---

[16] XLVIII (4 Gennaio, 1896), pp. 118-24.
[17] The sermon was printed in *Freeman's Journal,* April 3, 1897.

the *ralliement*. He approached young Abbé Félix Klein to smooth out the translation and prepare it for a French audience.[18] Abbé Klein shortened and improved the translation and wrote for it a vigorous preface in which he spoke of Father Hecker as an example of the priest of the future, a self-made man, a doctor of the spiritual life who understood that the modern man needed greater freedom. Hecker, he said, had insisted on more dependence on the direct inspiration of the Holy Spirit, on active rather than passive virtue, and desired to abolish the barriers that kept out the modern unbelievers from the Church. Chabrol and Klein arranged for a campaign of publicity to be given to the translation in the French press. Within a few weeks, the book went into three printings.

In Rome, O'Connell planned to translate the biography of Hecker into Italian, but when he was invited to give a paper at the Fourth International Scientific Congress at Fribourg from August 16 to 20, he wrote his paper on Father Hecker, making his idea of religious Americanism the chief theme in Hecker's life. He entitled his paper "A New Idea in the Life of Father Hecker". He distinguished between two kinds of Americanism. The political kind as found in the Declaration of Independence and the Constitution, he maintained, was fully consonant with Catholic doctrines. The other was ecclesiastical Americanism. The ideal relation between Church and State was union but that was the thesis which in practice was not possible; the hypothesis or practical solution was the freedom enjoyed by the Church in the United States. Hecker had accepted both Americanisms. Bishop Charles Turinaz of Nancy, a conservative, attacked O'Connell's paper and insisted that Hecker's ideas were really Protestant. He was answered by Klein who claimed that Turinaz had misinterpreted Hecker.

On November 7, 1897, a Jesuit, Father Coube, speaking at

[18] The French translation was *Le Père Hecker Foundateur des "Paulistes" Américains, 1819-1888*, par le Père W. Elliott, de la même Compagnie. Traduit et adapté de l'anglais avec autorization de l'auteur. Introduction par Mgr. Ireland. Préface par L'Abbé Félix Klein (Paris, 1897).

St. Sulpice, spoke of the four great evils that now threatened the Church: the Parliament of Religions, an article by Brunetière in *Revue des Deux Mondes,* Maurice Blondel's philosophy, and Father Hecker's Americanism. The following Sunday another Jesuit, Father Gaudeau, launched a similar attack on these evils. The term "Americanism" was now definitely attached to the movement but there were differences of opinion as to what the term signified. O'Connell's paper was printed in pamphlet form in both English and French and appeared in *La Quinzaine.*

There began to appear on March 3, 1898, in *La Verité,* a series of articles signed "Martel," who was Abbé Charles Maignen, a priest of the Society of the Brothers of Saint Vincent de Paul. The title of the first indicated the purpose of the series: "L'Américanisme Mystique." The articles examined critically the life of Father Hecker. Maignen accused Hecker of trying to make easy the approach of rationalists to the Church. He sneered at Hecker's preference for Anglo-Saxons and for democracy. In later articles, "Martel" attacked Monsignor O'Connell's paper at Fribourg and Keane's defense of the Parliament of Religion at Malines. Eventually, he called the biography of Hecker the symbol of a new school of theology, which he called "Americanism". He elaborated a plot of the Americanists against the Church in which the Parliament of Religions and the efforts to hold another in Paris were basic elements.

In May the essays were gathered in book form under the title, *Le Père Hecker est-il un Saint?* [19] When Cardinal Richard refused an imprimatur, a Roman publisher was obtained and the imprimatur secured from Père Albert Lepidi, O.P., the Master of the Sacred Palace. Superficially it seemed to have papal approval.

Maignen summed up the errors of Hecker: a belief in a natural aspiration to supernatural good; a distinction between the active and passive virtues; a wrong notion about the activity of the Holy Spirit; the elimination of the "customs house" for converts; an ignoring of the distinctions between precepts and counsels and opposing the religious life; a wrong notion of the spiritual life in

[19] *Études sur l'Américanisme Le Père Hecker est-il un Saint?*

his discussions of Latins and Anglo-Saxons; his advocating with Archbishop Ireland the separation of Church and State. Emphasizing the talk about Latins and Anglo-Saxons, the United States went to war with Spain on April 25 over Cuba. At the request of Cardinal Rampolla, Archbishop Ireland had tried to prevent the Spanish-American War, but his intervention came too late.

Maignen's book contained some new essays in which the Americanists were accused of certain liberalist doctrines in connection with Keane's speeches at the Parliament of Religions and an article by a "Romanus" in the *Contemporary Review.* Keane wrote to Rampolla, protesting the imprimatur given to Maignen's book. He also wrote an article in *Catholic World,* stating that his liberal ideas were the principles of Pope Leo. Americanism, he said, was just the sentiment of an American Catholic toward his country and had nothing to do with the ideas expressed in the book of Maignen.

Ireland complained to Rampolla that Maignen and Périès were defining Americanism in terms of French apostates and not in the words of real Americans. A move was made to put the French biography on the Index of Prohibited Books. In *La Verité* appeared some letters of Monsignor O'Connell distinguishing true Americanism and false Americanism. It was rumored that the pope had stopped the effort to put the biography on the Index and had appointed a commission of cardinals to examine the question of Americanism. Archbishop Ireland went to Rome and Cardinal Gibbons sent a letter protesting any papal action against Americanism. On February 7, Gibbons received a cablegram that his protest had come too late and Archbishop Ireland, arriving in Rome on January 31, was told that the letter against Americanism was already in the mails.

(b) *The Myth.* In his Apostolic Letter *Testem benevolentiae,*[20] the pope did not say that anyone held the reprobated doctrines which had been discussed in connection with the translation of the biography of Father Hecker. The doctrines of this Ameri-

[20] *American Ecclesiastical Review* XX (April, 1899), pp. 399-409.

canism were: that the Church should show indulgence to others in matters of doctrine and discipline; that external spiritual guidance was now superfluous because of a new abundance of the grace of the Holy Spirit; that natural virtues were better suited than supernatural virtues to the present day; that passive virtues were better in a former day but the active virtues were proper for the present times; that among the passive virtues those associated with the religious life were less well suited for the present day; that new ways should be adopted for bringing converts into the Church. But the pope added that the Americanism he reprobated did not include the characteristic qualities of the American people.

Archbishop Ireland and Archbishop Keane immediately insisted that they did not hold the condemned doctrines. The conservative opponents of Ireland, Archbishop Corrigan and Archbishop Messmer, thanked the pope for preserving the American Church from peril. But Cardinal Gibbons in his answer stated that no educated American Catholic held the condemned doctrines. Archbishop Ireland insisted that the pope had accepted his denial of the existence of the heresy and Cardinal Gibbons' answer was accepted in Rome, although it was never published in the cardinal's lifetime. The Americanism condemned in the papal document did have some resemblances to the theories and practices of the Americanism of Archbishop Ireland, Archbishop Keane, and Monsignor O'Connell, but the European Americanism was created by Maignen and expanded with statements of certain apostates and unnamed liberal Catholics of Europe. There was a third Americanism which was expressly exempted by the pope and that was the proper devotion of Americans to the American way of life and the American form of government.

The papal letter *Testem benevolentiae* ended any heretical Americanism, either European or American. When the chief Americanists, Archbishops Ireland and Keane, Monsignor O'-Connell, Abbé Klein and the Paulists denied that they held the doctrines which the pontiff had condemned, Maignen did not reassert the existence of the heresy. Americanization, the bone of contention in the United States, was not involved in the papal document. Abbé Klein in his autobiography called Americanism a "phantom heresy" and as it was described in the papal letter it was held by no one. The argument for political *ralliement* based on the progress of the Church in the democratic United States was indeed quieted, but that argument had little importance in the United States. Archbishop Ireland openly insisted that the real Americanism had not been touched by the papal letter, and before he left Europe in 1899 he explained to the press that the condemned Americanism was the creation of Abbés Périès and Maignen and had never really existed.

The major conflict within the United States during the European arguments over Americanism—the Americanization of Catholicism—was only accidentally touched by the papal letter. In the United States and in France the pontiff achieved his purpose in stopping the public controversy, but he did not really take sides in the bitter controversy over Americanization. The letter pleased the conservatives to some extent and wounded the progressives by uniting the word "Americanism" with reprobated doctrines; yet by exempting political Americanism from his criticism the pontiff had deprived the conservatives of victory and gave the Americanists a basis for saying that they had not been touched. The adaptation of Catholicism to the American milieu, which was the basic subject of the controversy in the United States, passed from a critical problem to a major source of friction between the same groups. Eventually, the followers of Archbishop Ireland were to triumph in the next two decades. In the failure of the conservatives' American Federation of Catholic Societies[21] and the temporary Roman suppression of the National Catholic Welfare Council in 1922 were evidences that the bitter feelings of the Americanist crisis were not yet dead even as late as the third decade of the 20th century.

[21] The strange story of this attempt by conservatives has been told in the unpublished thesis of Sister M. Gorman, "Federation of Catholic Societies in the United States, 1870-1920" (Notre Dame, 1962).

PART II
BIBLIOGRAPHICAL
SURVEY

Heiko Oberman/*Tübingen, W. Germany*

From Occam to Luther[*]

A Survey of Recent Historical Studies on the
Religious Thought of the 14th and 15th Centuries

IV

It is clearly impossible to reduce the late medieval critique of
pope and curia to philosophical nominalism in view of the extreme realism of Wyclif and Huss, not to mention the many
non-theological factors, such as the rising tide of nationalism and
the growing power of the town councils;[24] rather, theological
nominalism tried to provide for an ecumenical theology by
transcending the divisive school differences. The measure of its
failure is the continuation of Thomism and Scotism as alternative
options.

Two recent studies should be noted because they shed light on
the *via antiqua* in the later Middle Ages. The first deals with
the Dutch Thomist Heinrich van Gorkum[25]—of particular interest for Luther scholars since Louis Saint-Blancat showed in
his unpublished first book on Luther's glossen to Lombard's sen-

[*] This is the concluding section of a two-part article, the first part of
which appeared in *Concilium* 17.
[24] Cf. the valuable study by B. Moeller, *Reichsstadt und Reformation*
Gütersloh (1962), esp. pp. 55, 67.
[25] A. Weiler, *Heinrich von Gorkum (†1431): seine Stellung in der
Philosophie und der Theologie des Spätmittelalters* (Hilversum: Köln,
1962).

tences[26] that the copy used by Luther must have been one of the Basel editions by Nic. Kessler (1487, 1488, 1489, 1502, 1507) —namely the edition to which the *Conclusiones super IV libros sententiarum* of Heinrich were attached. Weiler comes to the conclusion that Heinrich is not of the same stature as Occam or Gerson (p. 305), but he adds: "Zweifellos ist es von grösster Bedeutung, dass gegenüber der arbiträren Weltanschauung Ockhams und der deterministischen Wyclifs die gemässigtrealistischen neuplatonisch gefärbten thomistischen Gedanken über die Strukturen von Kirche und Welt aufs neue laut werden" (p. 301). Yet Heinrich's *via utraque*—he studied both in Paris (1395-1419) and Cologne (1419-1431)—are reflected in his thought. The influence of Gerson's spirituality is notable and d'Ailly's ideas and terminology come through in the discussion of predestination; as investigator of the sisters of the common life in Cologne he comes to the conclusion: "Wenn das keine Lebensweise ist, nach der mit Recht jeder Christ Christo nachfolgen sollte, so habe ich nie die Heilige Schrift gelesen" (p. 48). But as a professor of theology involved in the clash between the *via antiqua* and the *via moderna*, Heinrich became known as *Thomistarum coloniensium monarcha* (p. 73).

Weiler has a higher regard for this renewal of Thomism than Ritter, which seems justified since Weiler is able to show that this Thomism is not a mere repristination[27] but a response to the actual theological problems of the times. This especially appears in Heinrich's interesting *Contra articulos Hussitarum,* less in the treatise *De sacramento altaris et efficacia missae,* but again clearly in the *Lectura super Evangelium.* Heinrich participates in the debate on Scripture and tradition of his time by insisting on the divine origin and authority of the "summi pontificis, cardinalium atque episcoporum decreta. . ." (p. 248); there is nowhere an indication that Heinrich would have had difficulties with the *"partim-partim"* formula of the last draft of the Tri-

---

[26] Microfilm deposited in Andover-Harvard Library.
[27] G. Ritter, *Via antiqua und Via Moderna auf den deutschen Universitäten des XV Jahrhunderts* (Darmstadt, 1963), esp. p. 136.

dentine decree. Whereas this book is important to our understanding of Cologne Thomism, which was to play such a fateful
role in the issue around Pfefferkorn and Reuchlin, the arduous
task suggested by the subtitle has not and could not have been
as satisfactorily executed, because a study of the alternatives to
late medieval Thomism, with the same love for detail and
empathy as invested in the analysis of Heinrich, would have required several volumes.

The second book which deals with the *via antiqua* in the 14th
and 15th centuries discusses the history of the heritage of John
Duns Scotus as regards the doctrine of divine *acceptation* in its
many implications.[28] Well known for his excellent dissertation
on the *acceptatio* doctrine of Duns Scotus,[29] Dettloff has now
pursued the history of this problem up to Luther, or, rather,
through the 15th century, including Gabriel Biel. Elsewhere I
have indicated [30] at what points critical questions have to be
raised; Duns Scotus is not only a point of reference but also the
standard of evaluation; hence new developments are regarded as
deviations. Dettloff finds in late medieval theology an "Entleerung
der Caritasvorstellung" (Robert Cowton, Petrus Aureoli, Occam,
Adam Wiidham, etc.); a "wachsende Übergewicht der potentia-
dei-absoluta Spekulationen" (Joh. de Bassolis, Occam); and
"die negative potentia-dei-absoluta-Spekulation . . . die einer
sehr schwerwiegenden Entstellung des Gottesbildes gleichkommt"
(Durandus, Petrus de Palude, Occam, Gabriel Biel) (pp.
362ff.).

It is a lasting contribution, however, to have pointed to the
intimate interaction between Scotism and nominalism which
makes it often almost impossible to determine whether an author

---

[28] W. Dettloff, *Die Entwicklung der Akzeptations—und Verdienstlehre
von Duns Scotus bis Luther mit besonderer Berücksichtigung der Fran-
ziskanertheologen* (Münster i. W., 1963).

[29] *Die Lehre von der acceptatio divina bei Johannes Duns Scotus mit
besonderer Berücksichtigung der Rechfertigungslehre* (Werl, 1954).

[30] Cf. my " 'Iustitia Christi' and 'Iustitia Dei': Luther and the Scholastic
Doctrines of Justification," in *Harv. Theol. Rev.* 59 (January, 1966), pp.
1-26.

is to be assigned to the school of Scotus or of Occam. With the exclusive interest in acceptation and merit, the problem of predestination does not sufficiently come into focus, though it is exactly this doctrine which differentiates between the two schools and which underlies systematically the other differences.[31] But Dettloff has given us a valuable collection of extensive quotations, many of them drawn from unpublished materials.

V

We conclude our survey[32] by pointing to a recent intensification of interest in the theology of Gabriel Biel. While under the direction of Hanns Rückert a critical edition of Biel's *Sentences Commentary* is being prepared by Wilfrid Werbeck, the first three volumes of the four-volume critical edition of the important *Canonis misse Expositio*[33] are now available. Among the

---

[31] Cf. my "Das tridentinische Rechtfertigungsdekret im Lichte der spätmittelalterliche Theologie," in *Zeitscher. f. Theol. Kirche* 61 (1964), pp. 251-282, esp. 267; "Duns Scotus, Nominalism and the Council of Trent," in *Johannes Duns Scotus*, eds. John K. Ryan and Bernardine M. Bonansea (Washington, D. C., 1965), pp. 311-344.

[32] We should mention here the survey of the present state of research *re* that fourth late medieval school, Augustinianism, by A. Zumkeller, *Analecta Augustiniana* 27 (1964), pp. 167-262. Jakobus Pérez of Valencia (d. 1490), here mentioned as an outstanding representative of the Augustinian school in the 15th century (p. 249), has lately been studied as the commentator on the Song of Songs by Reidlinger—*op. cit.*, n. 12, pp. 373ff.—and in an incisive monograph as commentator on the Psalms, by W. Werbeck, *Jacobus Pérez von Valencia, Untersuchungen zu seinem Psalmenkommentar* (Tübingen, 1959). In matters pertaining to justification closely related to Gregory of Rimini, Pérez proves to have a special place in the history of medieval hermeneutics by applying more consistently than Lyra all Psalms *ad litteram* to Christ (p. 127). An important contribution to this emerging field of interest is H. Hailperin, *Rashi and the Christian Scholars* (Pittsburgh, 1963), of which the whole second part (pp. 137-264 and pp. 282-358) is dedicated to Nicholas of Lyra (d. 1349), Rashi's (d. 1105) most eager student. Cf. H. de Lubac, *Exégèse Médiévale: les quatres sens de l'Ecriture* II (Paris, 1964), pp. 344-67, for a detailed discussion of the relation between Lyra and Thomas.

[33] Eds. H. Oberman and W. Courtenay: Band I (Wiesbaden, 1963); Band II (Wiesbaden, 1965); Band III (Wiesbaden, 1966). Vol IV is to contain an appendix *re* Biel's dependence on his predecessor in Mainz,

interpretive studies we mention first an analysis of Biel's doctrine of the eucharist.[34] Though it could have been written some three decades ago for the degree to which modern and especially non-German research is reflected—an Italian study on this very topic is not even mentioned [35]—we have here a careful sketch of Biel's discussion of the meaning of the eucharist according to his chief academic works. But beyond that it is interesting that a hitherto unknown early work (before 1449) of Biel, "Quaestiones metaphysicae", is adduced, in which, according to Damerau, transubstantiation, understood as the separation of accident and substance, is said to be possible only *de potentia Dei absoluta* (p. 107). This is so much in opposition to Biel's teaching in all his later works that we will suspend judgment until we see the promised edition of this treatise, which is elsewhere (p. 101) indicated as the product of the cooperation of a number of *magistri*. The significance of Biel's sermons on the eucharist is acknowledged (p. 102), but these do not function in the exposition.

The introduction to this exposition consists of a survey of the eucharistic teaching of Occam and his school, among which the sections on Nikolaus von Dinkelsbühl (d. 1433)[36] (pp. 76-94) and the Heidelberger *Gutachten* of 1451 (pp. 95-101) are deserving of our special interest. Damerau promises an edition of this *Gutachten* which will certainly clarify (and correct) his present quotations of selected passages. The author comes to the conclusion that faith and reason are radically divorced (pp. 106, 109, 244), that Biel is not a faithful disciple of Occam (p. 256), that the *potentia Dei ordinata* is undermined (p. 245),

---

Eggeling Becker of Braunschweig, and an extensive subject index intended to serve at the same time as a modern version of Johannes Altenstaig's *Vocabularius theologie* (Hagenau, 1517).

[34] R. Damerau, *Die Abendmahlslehre des Nominalismus insbesondere die des Gabriel Biel* (1964).

[35] P. Anatriello, *La Dottrina di Gabriele Biel sull'Eucaristia* (Milan, 1937).

[36] Cf. the detailed study of A. Madre, *Nikolaus von Dinkelsbühl, Leben und Werk* (Münster i. W., 1965).

and that the understanding of the sacraments as *causae sine qua non* implies "die Auflösung der bisher üblichen 'potentia dei ordinata' und die Gleichstellung des göttlichen Gnadenwirkens mit dem natürlichen" (*ibid.*). Whereas these traditional conclusions can be explained as due to the fact that the whole dimension of covenant theology within which Biel's arguments are anchorized has not been taken into account, the author is quite right in noting that Duns Scotus "wird zur zweiten Hauptautorität" (p. 247), that in Biel's *humiliatio* doctrine mystical "Gedankengut ist verarbeitet" (p. 249), and that a comparatively strong biblical orientation can be noted.

The relation between Biel and Luther—touched upon by Damerau in his last pages: "in der Reformation Luthers ist der echte Nominalismus . . . zum Durchbruch gekommen" (p. 258)— forms the subject matter of the important dissertation of Leif Grane, which carries the revealing inscription, taken from Luther's preface of 1545: "Quam verum est proverbium: Difficile est consueta relinquere. . . ." [37] From the point of view of late medieval research one might complain that only those sections in Biel are analyzed which function in Luther's early thought, especially in his *Disputatio contra scholasticam theologiam,* so that the organic and cohesive structure in the theology of late medieval thinkers cannot be uncovered. On the other hand, this mode of operation allows for a clear indication of the breaking points between Biel and Luther as seen from Luther's point of view: "Luthers verhältnis zum Ockhamismus ist ein historisches Problem, und der Ausgangspunkt für seine Behandlung sollte deshalb [?] bei Luther selbst gesucht werden" (p. 41).

Grane has seen very well that the Disputation concerns the "acquisition of love" (p. 222) and that Biel is one of the major Scholastic authorities attacked: "Der Text, der die Thesen gegen Biel hervorgerufen hat—*Collectorium* III d. 27 q. un. art 3.— ist ganz einfach das 'Skelett' der Disputation" (p. 47.). I am less

---

[37] *Contra Gabrielem. Luthers Auseinandersetzung mit Gabriel Biel in der Disputatio Contra Scholasticam Theologiam 1517.* Acta Theologica Danica IV (Gyldendal, 1962).

inclined to limit the scope of the *Disputatio* so radically to Gabriel Biel; the sources allow us to take Luther at his word that certain theses are directed against some of Biel's authorities, Scotus in particular; the last thesis against d'Ailly calls for an analysis of the *Canonis misse expositio*[38] where the question of the ethics of strict obedience to God, even to the point of *resignatio ad infernum,* is elaborately discussed.

After a brief survey (pp. 54-96) of Biel's theology, limited to the first three books of the *Collectorium*—a limitation defended on the grounds of Luther's Auseinandersetzung (p. 53, n. 5)— the author concludes *re* Biel, as Vignaux before him *re* Occam, that God's design underlying the justification of the sinner is sheer grace: "denn Gott kann mit seinem Geschöpf handeln, wie er will. Sein Willen ist der einzige formale Grund der Erlösung" (p. 96). Among the best parts of the book is the section on the *amor amicitiae* (pp. 224ff.) and the distinction between the *substantia actus* and the *intentio praecipientis* which is concluded with the complementary observation: "die Gesetzerfülling, zu der freie Wille ohne Hilfe der Gnade imstande ist, ist also eine Erfüllung, die von einer inneren moralischen Haltung bestimmt wird, obwohl die Zuordnung zu Gott aus Liebe fehlt" (p. 199). When one places these two quotations side by side one comes close to the intriguing notion that Biel's doctrine of justification is at once *sola gratia* and *solis operibus.*

In the assessment, Grane proves to differ from de Lagarde's and to contradict Damerau's final thesis: "keine zentraler Gedanke [Luthers] hat seinen Ursprung in der ockhamistischen Theologie, weder positiv noch negativ" (p. 380).[39] Though

[38] *Lect. 68, I;* critical edition, Vol. III (Wiesbaden, 1966), pp. 126ff.

[39] The same conclusion has been reached by F. Clark, S.J.: "The change from the theology of Gabriel Biel to that of Martin Luther was not an evolution but a revolution": *Eucharistic Sacrifice and the Reformation* (London, 1960), p. 322. Clark's main thesis is the defense of the orthodoxy of nominalistic theology as regards the sacrifice of the Mass and the eucharistic presence of Christ. By including extended translations of important late medieval sources this study does much to demythologize traditional "evaluations" of nominalistic theology. See esp. pp. 296ff., 365ff.

Grane quotes one of the relevant articles of Gerhard Ebeling[40] he could unfortunately not yet use the excellent first two parts of the new edition of Luther's first lectures on the Psalms[41] nor the dissertation of Reinhard Schwarz,[42] who carries the responsibility for the next double issue of *WA* 55, I and II. A closer analysis of the elaborate footnotes to this crucial part of the *initia Lutheri* would have allowed Grane to place his concluding thesis on a broader basis and formulate it in a more nuanced fashion. As a reaction against facile connections between Luther and the preceding late medieval tradition, Grane's study is a refreshing and valid correction.

VI

Surveying this review of the advances being made in late medieval studies, it appears that three major thrusts can be discerned.[43] First, one pursuing the history of exegesis with a marked interest in the rabbinic contribution (Smalley, Hailperin), through detailed investigations of biblical commentaries (Reidlinger, Werbeck), increasingly concerned with the methods of exegesis (de Lubac, Ebeling) and the theological principles underlying the postulated connection between the Old and New

[40] "Die Anfänge von Luthers Hermeneutik," in *Zeitsch. f. Theol. Kirche* 48 (1951), pp. 172-230.

[41] "Weimarer Ausgabe," 55, I, 1, Luthers 1. Psalmenvorlesung. Text der Glossen zu Ps. 1-15 mit Apparat. *WA* 55, II, 2. Text der Scholien zu Psalm 1-15 mit Apparat. Ed. by G. Pfeiffer and R. Schwarz unter Mitarbeit von G. Ebeling, L. Fendt (†), F. Hahn, A. Hamel (†), J. Heckel, H. Rückert, H. Volz, H. Wendorf (Weimar, 1963).

[42] *Fides, Spes und Caritas beim jungen Luther unter besonderer Berücksichtigung der mittelalterlichen Tradition* (Berlin, 1962). Though Schwarz makes a substantial contribution to our understanding of late medieval theology, this is so organically related to his analysis of the early Luther that it is more profitably discussed in a review article specially dedicated to that field. See G. Müller, *Kerygma und Dogma* (1965).

[43] For a discussion of pre-1962 publications not mentioned here, see my *Harvest of Medieval Theology* (Cambridge, Mass., 1963) with extensive bibliography (pp. 436-456). German edition *Spätscholastik und Reformation*. Band I. *Der Herbst der mittelalterlichen Theologie* (Zürich, 1965), pp. 398-413.

Testaments, the christological and tropological application (Werbeck, Ebeling). Whereas the first fruits of this line of research emerge in the field of Luther research by marking the importance of *WA* 55, I, 1 and 2, it is equally essential that the medieval tradition be traced through to the beginnings of the Counter-Reformation—e.g., to the first part of the *Aurea Rosa* (1503), by Silvester Prierias, O.P. (d. 1523), which is dedicated to a theology of exegesis.

Second, there is the continued concern with major doctrinal themes such as justification (Dettloff, Grane, Zumkeller, Douglass), Scripture and tradition (de Vooght), the eucharist (de Vooght, Damerau, Clark) carrying over into the study of pre-Tridentine theology (Clark) and that of the young Luther (Ebeling, Schwarz). While "institutional" history should not be neglected (Moeller), the clarification of the relation of Zwingli, Calvin and the representatives of the left wing of the Reformation to the medieval tradition calls for a vigorous and joint scholarly effort. Furthermore, the significance of the *via antiqua* has been brought into focus (Weiler); but there are no signs that we are about to reach a consensus as to the relation of the *via moderna* to the formation of Martin Luther (de Lagarde, Damerau, Clark, Grane). In addition to the need for the further edition of sources in this area, decisive progress can only be expected in the light especially of what we have designated as the first thrust, in conjunction with the yield of studies in area three.

Ecclesiology is here not included in the study of the traditional doctrinal *loci*. Because of the intense activity of scholars in this area and the new perspectives opening up in recent years—not unrelated to the stark contrast between the first and the second Pope John XXIII—we are inclined to discern here a third promising thrust in late medieval scholarship. Striking advances have been made through the study of canon law, especially of the 12th-century decretists (Tierney); pursuing the concerns of Otto von Gierke, *Das Deutsche Genossenschaftsrecht,* esp. Part III— originally published in 1881 this gigantic work had to be made available again (Darmstadt 1954)—not only the legal and philosophical but also the theological aspects of political thought have been analyzed (Ullman, Wilks, Morisson). Through a fresh effort to evaluate particular views of the Church not according to timeless standards, but in the context of the actual historical challenges such as the emergency situation caused by a schism—1130, 1159, 1378, 1409—(Classen, Franzen, Posthumus Meyjes), a new openness toward conciliar ideas can be noted with the tendency to distinguish between "true" and "false" conciliarism or between "conciliar" and "conciliaristic" thought (Tierney, Franzen); though not all scholars in the field are willing to rehabilitate the "Fathers of Constance", d'Ailly and Gerson (de Vooght), there is a clear trend to mark Occam as the culprit (Tierney, Posthumus Meyjes, de Lagarde) and associate him closely with Marsilius of Padua. As we suggested in the discussion of de Lagarde's work, there is reason to believe that a further study of the relation of Occam to Marsilius and to the several types of conciliarism represented at the Council of Basle (1431-1449) and even at the Fifth Lateran Council (1512-1517) will affect this evaluation. In a next stage it will be important to continue this ecclesiological compound of canon law and conciliar research into the early 16th century. It is by no means certain that in a discussion, thus oriented, of the treatises exchanged in the period 1518-1520 between the theological advisor of Pope Leo X, Prierias, and Luther, the first would prove to be more true to what is now emerging as "orthodox" conciliar thought.

Confronted with these various research tasks in the several areas of major concern, it seems clear that the walls erected between medieval and (Counter-) Reformation studies, strengthened by the establishment of separate chairs in the academic departments of history and Church history, are artificial obstacles which tend to obscure the continuity in this period by separating what history has put together.

PART III
DOCUMENTATION
CONCILIUM

Office of the Executive Secretary
Nijmegen, Netherlands

Béda Rigaux, O.F.M. / *Brussels, Belgium*

St. Peter in Contemporary Exegesis

The person, the history and the primacy of St. Peter are important and much discussed topics in contemporary exegesis.[1] The text of Matthew 16, 18-19 is the focal point of discussion and disagreement. It has caused more than one person to lose his composure, and one cannot ask

---

[1] For an overall perspective and a general bibliography see: O. Linton, *Das Problem der Urkirche in der neueren Forschung: Eine kritische Darstellung* (Uppsala, 1932); F. M. Braun, *Aspects nouveaux du problème de l'Eglise* (Fribourg, 1942): revised and expanded in a German edition, *Neues Licht auf die Kirche: Die protestantische Kirchendogmatik in ihrer neuesten Entfaltung* (Einsiedeln, 1946); R. Baumann, *Des Petrus Bekenntnis und Schlüssel* (Stuttgart, 1950); *ibid., Fels der Welt: Kirche des Evangeliums und Papsttum* (Tübingen, 1956); O. Cullmann, *Petrus: Jünger, Apostel, Märtyrer. Das historische und das theologische Petrus problem* (Stuttgart, ²1960); A. Penna, *S. Pierre* (Paris, 1958); J. Betz, *Christ-Petra-Petrus (Kirche und Ueberlieferung. Festschrift J. R. Geiselmann)* (Freiburg im Br., 1960), pp. 1-21; F. Obrist, *Echtheitsfragen und Deutung der Primatsstelle Mt 16, 18ff in der Deutschen Protestantischen Theologie der letzten dreissig Jahre* (Münster, 1960); J. Ringger, *Petrus der Fels: Das Felsenwert. Zur Sinndeutung von Mt 16, 18, vor allem im Lichte der Symbolgeschichte* (Begegnung der Christen. Studien evang. und kathol. Theologen, ed. M. Roesle-O. Cullmann) (Stuttgart-Frankfurt, ²1960), pp. 271-347; J.-L. D'Aragon, "Bibliographie sur l'Eglise dans la Bible," in *L'Eglise dans la Bible: Communications présentées à la XVII réunion annuelle de l'Abebac* (Brussels-Paris, 1962), pp. 169-202; B.-M. Metzger, *Index to Periodical Literature on Christ and the Gospels* (Leiden, 1966); A.-J. Mattil, Jr.-M. Bedford Mattil, *A Classified Bibliography of Literature on the Acts of the Apostles* (Leiden, 1966), nn. 3585-3660; A. Vögtle, "Petrus," in *Lex. Theol. und Kirche*, 8 (1963), pp. 334-40.

any reporter to remain absolutely neutral on such a heady issue. However, a reporter should be as objective as possible.

My task here, then, is to delineate the present status of the research being done on this question, to point out the developing lines of convergence and the points where opinions diverge. To give a complete account would require a full-sized book. So this article will select various materials that give us an idea of the principal positions being maintained today.

Now the fact is that we would falsify the outlook of contemporary exegesis if we restricted ourselves to the question of Peter's primacy. This question is actually part of a much larger context within which it becomes a proper and meaningful question. The conception which the primitive Church had about herself, her view of what Jesus thought about her mission and her work, are the fundamental and decisive issues. "To understand the New Testament ministry, one must consider the background against which it developed: the whole New Testament outlook on the world and its faith in Christ's mission." [2]

For this reason, the present study is divided into two parts: (1) the concept of the Church that was held by the primitive community and by Jesus himself; (2) St. Peter and his primacy.

I

THE CONCEPT OF THE CHURCH

In former days the Church was viewed as a collection of individuals who were bound together by their common adherence to Christ's teaching. More recently, three new points have come to light. (1) The new economy replaces the old one; present-day studies focus on two points—the "Son of Man" (Dan. 7, 9-28) and the "remnant" mentioned by the prophets. (2) The notion

[2] O. Linton, "Kirche und Amt im Neuen Testament," in A. Nyrgten, *En Bruch von der Kirche* (Göttingen, 1961), p. 143; E. Dinkler, "Die Petrus-Rom Frage: Ein Forschungsbericht," in *Theol. Rundschau* 25 (1959), p. 195: "A discussion of the Matthaean text, restricted solely to the problem of Peter, is not fruitful."

of the kingdom is central in the preaching of Jesus; what then is the relationship between the Church and this present and future kingdom of which Christ spoke? (3) In the Church there developed a clear awareness of being the new People of God. Thus there is a correlation between the kingdom and this new people. Was Jesus responsible for the transition from the former to the latter?

1. Old and New Covenant

The relationship between the old and the new economy became an object of theological reflection in the early Church. The people of the Old Testament were God's own community (Dt. 32, 2ff.; 1 Chr. 28, 8; Neh. 13, 1; Mi. 2, 58; Jgs. 20, 2). This idea was carried over to the New Testament community, which was called the "community of God" (Acts 20, 28; 1 Cor. 1, 2; 10, 32; 11, 22; 2 Cor. 1, 1) or simply "the community" (Acts 9, 31; 1 Cor. 12, 28).[3] Israel was also the People of God, and this notion is picked up in the New Testament. It is stated explicitly in 1 Pt. 2, 9-10, and other texts (2 Cor. 6, 10; Heb. 8, 10; Apoc. 21, 3) attest to it.

The problem posed by present-day exegesis is more specific. Linking Daniel 7, 9-28 to Chapter 53 of Deutero-Isaia, F. Kattenbusch[4] asserts that one cannot talk about the Son of Man without connecting his people with him, for he is a symbol of them. For Kattenbusch, Daniel is "the source for the concept of the Church". Thus Jesus would have wanted to establish a synagogal community apart from Israel. And that is why a new cult was born in Jesus' community at the Last Supper.

A similar conclusion is reached by K.-L. Schmidt,[5] who analyzes the concept of the "remnant". When Israel rejects Jesus,

[3] Cf. N. Dahl, *Das Volk Gottes: Eine Untersuchung zum Kirchenbewusstsein der Urchristentums* (Oslo, 1941), pp. 2-50; H. Strathmann, "Ekklesia," in *Theol. Wörterbuch z. N.T.* 4, pp. 32-39.

[4] F. Kattenbusch, "Der Quellort der Kirchenidee," in *Festgabe für A. v. Harnack* (Tübingen, 1921), pp. 142-72.

[5] K.-L. Schmidt, "Die Kirche des Urchristentums," in *Festgabe für A. Deissmann* (Tübingen, 1927), pp. 251-319.

he detaches himself from the People of God to lay the foundation for a new People of God. Thus Matthew 16, 18-19 should be re-integrated into the larger context of Jesus' overall activity.

Oepke[6] reconstructs it a little differently. As K.-L. Schmidt presents it, the establishment set up by Jesus looks too much like a group set up within the bosom of Judaism. Schmidt does not seem to have paid enough attention to Jesus' words: "I shall build my Church." Due attention must be paid to the real meaning of "build" and, in particular, to "my Church", which designates a specific new reality. Hence Oepke would revise Schmidt's theory. One must take serious account of the eschato-logical aspect of the establishment of the Church. One must situ-ate it once again within the definitive act of salvation and recog-nize the true dimensions of Jesus' claim about the fate of Israel as a whole. The Master proposes to fashion a new people, to contract a new covenant, and to make a new beginning. When Israel rejects this message and spurns its Messiah, it performs an act of secession and becomes a synagogue; the kingdom of God passes over to those Jews who believe in Christ and to all the nations of the world. That is how the Church is born. She is not a formally structured institution, but she is an institution clearly attested to by the image of "building". Oepke's view has had a profound impact which is still felt in present-day exegesis.[7]

[6] A. Oepke, "Der Herrenspruch über die Kirche (Mt 16, 17-19) in der neuesten Forschung," in Studia Theologica (1948-49), pp. 110-65; Idem, Das neue Gottesvolk in Schriftum, Schauspiel, bildende Kunst und Weltgestaltung (Gütersloh, 1950).

[7] N. Dahl, "The Parable of Growth," in Studia Theologica 5 (1951), pp. 132-166; R. Flew, Jesus and His Church: A Study of the Idea of the Ecclesia in the New Testament (London, ²1953); J. Horst, "Der Kirchengedanke bei Mt 16, 18," in Zeitschrift für syst. Theol. 20 (1943), pp. 127-45; E. Stauffer, Die Theologie des Neuen Testaments (Güters-loh, ⁴1948); O. Cullmann, Saint Pierre, pp. 167-174; P. Nepperchristen-sen, "Wer hat die Kirche gestiftet?" in Symb. Bibl. Ups. 12 (1955), pp. 23-35; D. Miller, The People of God: About the Basic New Testament Account of the Origin and Nature of the Church (London, 1959); I. Backes, "Die Kirche ist das Volk Gottes des Neuen Bundes," in Trierer Theol. Zeitschrift 69 (1960), pp. 116-17; Ibid., "Gottes Volk im Neuen Bunde," in Trierer Theol. Zeitschrf. 70 (1961), pp. 80-93.

2. Kingdom of God and Church

In short we may say that the new exegetical outlook has posed the historical problem in its true light. Did Jesus' preaching about the kingdom of God contain an announcement about a community which would be organized into a Church? Note that there is no question of trying to prove that the Church existed during Jesus' lifetime; the Church was born on Pentecost. Moreover, the Church cannot be identified with the covenant and the kingdom, because their aims go beyond the boundaries of community.

Getting back to the question we have just asked, we should now consider the view of W. G. Kümmel. Kümmel's answer is an emphatic "no", and it is based on the eschatological notions entertained by Jesus.[8] As he sees it, Jesus foretold the full consummation of the kingdom within a generation, and was mistaken in this. The Church is a product of the faith which was born out of Jesus' death and resurrection. The authority of this author, his deep knowledge of the problem and his clear presentation have lent great weight to his exegetical position. According to him, the twelve apostles and the disciples of Jesus never regarded themselves as a new people; Oepke's thesis is untenable. In like manner, one cannot accept the view of those who see the "remnant" in Jesus' little community. And we might note in passing that Kümmel's resistance to the "remnant" approach has been backed up by others—Bultmann, Oepke himself, and particularly J. Jeremias.[9]

Kümmel admits that Jesus claimed to be the Messiah, but

[8] W. Kuemmel, "Kirchenbegriff und Erfüllung: Untersuchung zur eschatologischen Verkündigung Jesu," in *Symb. Bibl. Ups.* 1 (1943); Idem, *Heissung und Erfüllung: Untersuchungen zur eschatologischen Verkündigung Jesu* (Zurich, ²1953); Idem, "Jesus und die Anfänge der Kirche," in *Studia Theologica* 7 (1953), pp. 1-27 (*Heilsgeschehen und Geschichte* [Marburg, 1965], pp. 289-309); Idem, "Die Naherwartung in der Verkündigung Jesu," in *Zeit und Geschichte: Dankesgabe an R. Bultmann* (Tübingen, 1964), pp. 31-46 (*Heilsgeschehen*, pp. 457-70).

[9] R. Bultmann, *Theol. Bläter* 20 (1941), pp. 274; A. Oepke, *op. cit.*, p. 140, n. 5; p. 165, n. 1; J. Jeremias, "Der Gedanke des 'Heiligen Reste' im Spätjudentum und in der Verkündigung Jesu," in *Zeitschr. für neut. Wiss.* 42 (1949), p. 184.

that does not mean that he gathered a community around himself. Moreover, even if he foresaw that there would be a brief
time interval between the resurrection and the parousia, he
made no provisions to translate the expectations of the faithful
into a Church; nothing in the texts proves that Jesus had any
idea about the existence of a group separated from Israel and
including all the nations of the world. Analysis of Matthew 16,
18 is not at all conclusive. Only one thing establishes a link between Jesus and the Church: the group which was around Jesus
before his death found new reason to maintain its existence afterward because of its faith in the resurrection. It is the relationship of Jesus himself to the community, not any words of his,
that forms the connecting link.

Kümmel's thesis has been severely criticized by some exegetes
in the Protestant camp—e.g., O. Cullmann, R. Bohren, and
J.-L. Klink.[10] The Scandinavian exegetes open up new perspectives. Anton Fridrichsen maintains that the preaching of Jesus
about the kingdom of God forces one to say that from the very
beginning he went beyond Judaic notions and his ideas led up to
the Church. The hopeful expectation of Israel and the fulfillment
of the Law are themes picked up by Jesus; he makes his own
person and his work the central points of these themes, and his
work is the Church which was established by his blood.[11] O.
Linton is the one who has spelled out this line of thought most
fully, providing us with an analysis and a justification of the
New Testament ministry. This ministry is a participation in the
service and the authority of Jesus; it is marked by a deep accord
with Christ and the Holy Spirit, and it includes service to one's
brothers.[12] G. Lindeskog stresses the fact that Jesus did announce

[10] O. Cullmann, "Kirchenbegriff und Kirchenbewusstsein in der Urgemeinde und bei Jesus," in *Theol. Zeitschrift* 1 (1945), pp. 146-47; R.
Bohren, *Das Problem der Kirchenzucht im Neuen Testament* (Zurich,
1952), p. 30, n. 2; J.-L. Klink, *Het Petrustype in het Nieuwe Testament
en de Oud-Christelijke Letterkunde* (Leiden, 1947).
[11] A. Fridrichsen, *Messias und Kirche: Ein Buch von der Kirche*
(Göttingen, 1951), pp. 45-48.
[12] O. Linton, "Kirche und Amt im Neuen Testament," in *Ein Buch
von der Kirche* (Göttingen, 1951), pp. 110-44.

the kingdom and build a community, even if the New Testament does not clearly affirm the bond between kingdom and Church.[13]

On the Catholic side, several studies have broached the problem of Jesus and the Church. The contributions of O. Kuss and J. Betz are among the most fundamental.[14] However, it is A. Vögtle who has taken up the question within the context of present-day exegetical positions and problems.[15] The Fribourg scholar believes that Kümmel's criticism of his predecessors is legitimate, but that the problem is more complicated than Kümmel would have us believe. It is true, of course, that we must distinguish the ecclesiology of the post-resurrection Church from the outlook of Jesus himself. Moreover, the Church appears to be of divine foundation, to be a Church of God. Finally, the notion of Church is one whose origins are to be sought in the post-resurrection community. Vögtle then takes up a critical analysis of Matthew 16, 18.

He admits that the concepts of "People of God" and "remnant" are not enough to enable us to say that Jesus founded a Church. But considering how the Jews misunderstood and rejected Jesus, we can easily picture Jesus looking ahead to a time when his disciples and apostles would be all alone. Thus one could say— and Kümmel does not deny this—that Jesus explained the meaning of his death and resurrection to a small circle of followers because he pictured this eventuality. It is here that the new People of God was born. It did not grow up alongside the Old Covenant; instead it effectuated a new covenant on the basis of a new salvation.

Now this does not mean that one can interpret Christ's words about the kingdom as comments on the Church. To repeat once

---

[13] G. Lindeskog, "Gottes Reich und Kirche im N.T.," *ibid.*, pp. 145-57. O. Michel, *Das Zeugnis des Neuen Testaments von der Gemeinde* (1941).

[14] O. Kuss, "Jesus und die Kirche im N.T.," in *Theol. Quart.* 135 (1955), pp. 28-55; Idem, *Auslegung und Verkündigung* (Regensburg, 1963), pp. 25-77; J. Betz, "Die Gründung der Kirche durch den historischen Jesus," in *Theol. Quart.* 138 (1958), pp. 152-83.

[15] A. Vögtle, "Jesus und die Kirche," in *Begegnung der Christen,* pp. 54-81.

more: the kingdom is not the Church. It lies beyond the Church, both by its very nature and in its ultimate goals. It is also futile to try to establish a link between Jesus and the Church on the basis of the "Son of Man" concept, whether it be interpreted as an individual or a group. The preaching of the Gospel to the pagans does not shed a decisive light on the question either. Hence the relationship between Jesus and Church must be determined on the basis of two established facts. Jesus did not speak in public about the need for him to undergo an expiatory death. Rejected by the Jews, misunderstood by Israel, he was constrained to limit his revelation of a new state to the group of apostles; and it was at the Last Supper that he announced the new covenant founded on his own blood.

This assumes that Jesus was figuring there would be a span of time between the resurrection and the parousia. Hence the words of Matthew 16, 18 could well have been spoken by Jesus. It is evident, then, that Vögtle has cleared away some of the debris, enabling us to reconstruct a situation where the text of Matthew can be integrated with the known views of Jesus. R. Schnackenburg presents a position that is quite close to that of Vögtle (in his two fine works).[16]

With masterly skill, B. C. Butler (now the auxiliary bishop of London) presents us with another side of the picture. Speaking at the Second International Convention on New Testament Studies (Oxford 1961), he delivered a distinguished paper on "Spirit and Institution in the New Testament".[17] Christianity is a spiritual message which Jesus addressed not to isolated individuals, but to the Jewish community as a whole. But it is undeniable that this community rejected the Good News and its preacher. This break between Jesus and his people did not alter his messianic pretensions. As the Messiah, he would have to manifest himself to a new people; the Twelve and the disciples were the embryo of

---

[16] R. Schnackenburg, *Gottesherrschaft und Reich: Eine biblisch-theologische Studie* (Freiburg im Br., ⁴1965); Idem, *Die Kirche im N. T.* (*Quaestiones disputatae*, 14) (Freiburg im Br., ³1963).

[17] B. Butler, *Spirit and Institution in the N.T.* (*Studia Evangelica*, III) (Berlin, 1964), pp. 138-65.

this new people. By rejecting the Messiah, the chosen people lost their raison d'être and were replaced by a new election and a new covenant. The death of God's messenger would toll the knell of the Jewish community itself.

Its disappearance, however, forced Jesus to establish a new community. His life was menaced, but somehow he had to insure permanence to his message. The resurrection would represent victory for both the message and the messenger. Thus the "dialectical moment" in the ministry of Jesus is the selection, training, mission and power of the Twelve, and also the promise that they will be "judges over the twelve tribes of Israel". Now since every community requires some minimum of organization, the Twelve were destined to become the leaders of this new community. The resurrection gave new strength and identity to the Messiah's disciples. Through them and around them was organized the preaching of the new message and the new cult.

It is in this framework that we must interpret Matthew 16, 18. Just as obedience to God is founded on the rock of Jesus' Word (Mt. 7, 25; Lk. 6, 18), so the new community is founded on a "rock". Furthermore, Jesus is not a Greek thinker; he is a son of Judaism and he thinks in Jewish terms. To insure continuity to his message and to the salvation it proclaims, he must work through a community. Hence institutionalism was included in the presuppositions of our Lord's ministry, and it was incorporated in the results which followed from this ministry.

If, like Schnackenburg,[18] we try to sum up the relationship between Jesus and the Church in terms of the history of his ministry, we find a Catholic *consensus* on the following points. To begin with, we are justified in saying that (1) Jesus' preaching about the kingdom and his messianic claims resulted in a new covenant; (2) the gathering around Jesus (of those who awaited the kingdom and followed Jesus) is contrasted with those who constituted "the lost sheep of the house of Israel" (Mt. 10, 6; cf. Mk. 6, 34); (3) this contrast is heightened by

[18] R. Schnackenburg, "Kirche: I. Die Kirche im N.T.," in *Lex. Theol. und Kirche* 6 (1961), pp. 167-69.

the fact that, unlike the Pharisees and Essenes, Jesus addressed himself to sinners, to *all*. It is not a question of a community set apart, but of a new People of God which is to replace those who have proved false (Mk. 2, 17; Mt. 11, 28-30; 21, 31-32); (4) Jesus' summons was rejected, but the plan of God will be realized anyway (Mk. 4, 11-12); Jesus foresees his death and forecasts it to his disciples; it is to be a death "for many" (Mk. 14, 24), without any distinction between Jews and pagans; this is the way the notion of the new covenant is elaborated; (5) Jesus foresaw that after his death his disciples would not wait in lonely isolation for the end to come; they would unite and form a community, following up the demands and the promises of Jesus.

This last proposition acquires its meaning and value from the actions of Jesus which establish the Church: (1) gathering followers who will be the true Israel; (2) forming a group, the Twelve, who will replace Israel (Mt. 19, 28; Lk. 22, 30); (3) abandoned by the masses and the leaders of Israel, Jesus continues to bring the Twelve into union with his own life, his own destiny, and his salvific intentions. He gives them special instruction and prepares them for his own death. The institution of the eucharist at the Last Supper includes the post-resurrection situation (Mt. 22, 16. 20. 30).

3. *Jesus the Messiah—the Twelve*

These conclusions become very shaky indeed if no stand is taken on the radical proposals of the post-Bultmann exegetes who tackle two major points.

The most radical exegetes deny that Jesus had any messianic pretensions. As we know, this is one of the pivotal points in the thought of Bultmann himself. Bornkamm has modified this position to a considerable degree, without going so far as to admit that Jesus presented himself as the Messiah.[19] Tödt, on the other hand, claims that Jesus did not even claim the title or the function of the "Son of Man".[20] One frequently finds that Tödt's

---

[19] G. Bornkamm, *Jesus von Nazareth* (Stuttgart, 1959).
[20] H. Tödt, *Der Menschensohn in der synoptischen Ueberlieferung*

position is taken for granted in current studies. However, in the works of Schnackenburg and Rigaux one can find reasons which show that this view is ill-founded.[21]

On the other hand, the same exegetical school will not even admit that Jesus gathered "Twelve" around him. G. Klein and W. Schmithals discuss this question in two important articles.[22] They come out in opposition to another group of exegetes who do admit that Jesus set up a group of Twelve: K. H. Rengstorf, O. Cullmann, N. A. Dahl, A. Wikenhauser, H. Riesenfeld.[23] Another current of thought is presented by A. von Harnack, A. Friedrichsen, J. Munck, H. Mosbech and E. Lohse. They say that the disciples were not named apostles at the beginning of the early Church, that this came about under the influence of Paul, that the Twelve never formed an institution.

W. Schmithals has tried to show that one must start with Paul's idea of the apostolate. It is an error to make a distinction between two different types of apostles: in the strict sense, the

(Gutersloh, 1959). See review by J. Sint, "Der Menschensohn in der synoptischen Ueberlieferung," in *Zeitschrift für kath. Theol.* 85 (1961), pp. 221-29. The problem of the historicity of Jesus has spawned so many publications that we cannot list them here. For a review of recent literature see W. Kümmel, "Jesusforschung seit 1950," in *Theol. Rundschau* 31 (1966), pp. 39-53; *idem*, "Der persönliche Anspruch Jesu und der Christusglaube der Urgemeinde," in *Marburg. Theol. Stud.* 3 (1965), pp. 429-38. On the present status of the problem, cf. B. Rigaux, "L'historicité de Jésus devant l'exégèse récente," in *Rev. bibl.* 65 (1958), pp. 481-522; J. Geiselmann, *Jesus der Christus: Die Frage nach dem Historischen Jesus* (Munich, 1965). This can be complemented by Ph. Vielhauer, "Jesus und der Menschensohn," in *Zeitschr. für Theol. Kirche* 60 (1963), pp. 133-177; F. Borsch, "The Son of Man," in *Anglic. Theol. Rev.* 45 (1963), pp. 174-90; reply to Vielhauer in M. Black, "The Son of Man: Problem in Recent Research and Debate," in *Bull. J. Rylands Libr.* 45 (1963), pp. 305-08; W. Kümmel, "Der persönliche Anspruch Jesu und der Christusglaube der Urgemeinde," in *Marburg Theol. Stud.* 1 (1963), pp. 1-10.

[21] R. Schnackenburg, *Gottesherrschaft und Reich,* pp. 113-15; B. Rigaux, "La seconde venue de Jésus," in *La Venue du Messie* (Paris-Brussels, 1964), pp. 201-02.

[22] G. Klein, *Die Zwölf Apostel: Ursprung und Gehalt einer Idee* (Göttingen, 1961); W. Schmithals, *Das Kirchliche Apostelamt: Eine Historische Untersuchung* (Göttingen, 1961).

[23] Discussion and citations in B. Gerhardson, "Die Boten und die Apostel," in *Svensk Exegetish Årsbok* 27 (1963), pp. 89-131.

Twelve and Paul; in the broad sense, the disciples which were so called by Paul. The distinction came about under the influence of Gnostic-Iranian ideas, which resulted in the concept of the group of Twelve around 120-150. Peter held first place in the Synoptic gospels because he was the first to have a vision of the resurrected Christ. The longing for the parousia creates the hope of seeing the Twelve ruling over the twelve tribes of Israel. But this notion of the Twelve was ephemeral; when Paul returns to Jerusalem for the first time, the group had already disappeared. The Twelve were made the authentic eyewitnesses for apologetical and polemical purposes. It is only around 100 that the Twelve became the twelve apostles.[24]

Klein acknowledges the importance of Schmithals' work, but he feels that the hypothesis of Gnostic influence on the whole notion of the apostolate is a very tentative one. In his view, the Pauline type of apostolate is not connected with Jesus at all; it is the work of Barnabas. In the middle of the 2nd century A.D., 2 Peter and the gospel of Luke (the work of some anonymous author) connected the apostolate with the Master. Thus it was this anonymous author who created the notion of the apostolate.

B. Gerhardson characterizes this two-pronged exegetical attack as "the most radical position within the radical Bultmannian camp". He criticizes these exegetes for their gratuitous skepticism toward the sources and their questionable exploitation of them. He feels these exegetes have an exaggerated confidence in their own ideas, too readily dismiss the views of others, and are totally unrealistic in their historical reconstruction of the primitive community and its underlying traditions. As a case in point, Galatians

[24] We must distinguish the use of the word "apostle" from the appointment of the Twelve, and the appointment itself from the de facto existence of a group of twelve. See J. Dupont, *Le Nom d'Apôtre a-t-il été donné aux Douze par Jésus?* (Louvain, 1956); B. Rigaux, "Die 'Zwölf' in Geschichte und Kerygma," in *Der historische Jesus und der kerygmatische Christus: Beiträge zum Christus-verständnis in Forschung und Verkündigung* (Berlin, 1960), pp. 468-86; N. Van Bohemen, "L'institution des Douze: Contribution à l'étude des relations entre l'évangile de Matthieu et celui de Marc," in *La Formation des Evangelles* (Paris, 1957), pp. 116-51.

1 presumes some type of investiture such as that which is presented in Matthew 16, 17-19.[25]

On the Catholic side exegetes have not failed to vindicate the historicity of Mark 3 and to devote their attention to the term "apostolos". Monsignor Cerfaux has analyzed its components in his usual authoritative fashion. So we find ourselves once again confronted with the critical Matthaean text.

II
MATTHEW'S TEXT

Matthew 16, 18 can only be seen in its true light when it is placed within the framework of the whole New Testament tradition.[25a]

1. *Peter in New Testament Tradition*

We shall not spend time discussing the preponderant place accorded to Peter in New Testament tradition. Aside from a few details which do not change the overall image, the exegetes find themselves in agreement on this picture, even though they may not draw the same conclusions. Therefore, we shall devote our attention to some of the important and controversial points.

The Acts of the Apostles presents us with a Peter who is acting as the head of the primitive community. He is the most important person in this community and he is its spiritual leader. He is at work not only in Jerusalem but also in Samaria and Caesarea, before moving on to "another place" (Acts 12, 1-19). Notice that Peter not only has a responsible position in the internal affairs of the Jerusalem community, but he also inspects the missionary work being done in Samaria (8, 14ff.) and brings pagans into the Church (10, 1-48).

[25]B. Gerhardson, *Die Boten und die Apostel*, pp. 89-131; *Idem, Memory and Manuscript: Oral Tradition and Written Transmission in Rabbinic Judaism and Early Christianity* (Uppsala, 1961), pp. 182-87.

[25a] We must agree with O. Kuss, *op. cit.,* p. 38, n. 25: There is still an urgent need for a Catholic book on Peter that would take full account of the questions posed by modern exegesis and biblical criticism."

This post-resurrection situation corresponds with the image of Peter presented in the Synoptic gospels.[26] He is the first one called (Mk. 1, 16-17); he belongs to a privileged quartet composed of himself, Andrew, James and John. His name is placed first on every listing of the apostles. He is the spokesman and representative.

The portrait of his personality and outlook is the same in all the Synoptic gospels. He is generous, loyal and obliging, but he is also impulsive, rash and fallible. None of the Synoptics try to gloss over his betrayal of Christ during the passion, although the story is retouched a little bit. Jesus gives him a special role, addressing the other apostles through him; this corresponds to his role as spokesman, which is generally acknowledged. Only critical or confessional bias would lead someone to deny or minimize Peter's special position.[27]

The gospel of Saint John follows the same vein. Despite its mention of the important role of the "beloved disciple", it acknowledges right at the start that Jesus gave Peter the name of Rock (1, 42), and it stresses the decisive confession of Peter (6, 67-69).

The first critical problem is the conferral of a surname on Simon, which makes his name "Peter". This change of name from Simon to Peter deserves close consideration, and it has been given this consideration by such exegetes as W. G. Kümmel and Oscar Cullmann.[28] "Petros" appears 154 times in the New Testament; "Simon" appears 75 times: "Kephas" appears 9 times, 8 of these in St. Paul who never uses "Simon" and only twice uses "Petros". The word "Kephas" has been the subject of so many studies that we could not begin to detail them in this brief treatment. In the light of the studies made by Ringger, Clavier and J.

---

[26] See J. Schmid, "Petrus 'der Fels' und die Petrusgestalt der Urgemeinde," in *Begegnung der Christen: Festschrift O. Karrer* (Frankfurt, 1959), pp. 347-359.

[27] E. Dinkler feels that Matthew 16, 17ff. is a *vaticinum ex eventu* and a creation of the community. Hence he concludes that the whole synoptic tradition on Peter's preeminence must be attributed to the community. We say this by way of reminder, because no proof is adduced.

[28] O. Cullmann, *Pierre,* p. 22; E. Dinkler, *Petrus,* pp. 186-87.

Betz,[29] we can assert that it is an Aramaean and not a Hebrew word.

The first question is that of *gender*. Dell concluded that it was feminine.[30] The principal argument was based on the fact that in Syriac the corresponding "Kepha" was feminine. From this he inferred that the change of gender in Greek (Petros-Petra) in Matthew 16, 18 could only be a citation of the Greek Church. Others held the view that the Aramaean word itself could be both masculine and feminine.[31] On the basis of the Palestinian and Samaritan targums, exegesis has acknowledged that the word is masculine.[32] Thus the possibility is open that, in Aramaean, Kephas could be made an epithet for a man.

The second question concerns the word's *meaning*. Does "Kephas" mean "stone" or "rock"? The choice is important. If Simon is a stone, he could be one stone among the other stones. Ringger insists on the fact that in the Aramaean targums "Kepha" always means "Rock".[33] But even today some exegetes choose "Peter" rather than "Rock", or remain undecided like Lagrange.[34]

One must respect the objectivity of Clavier who wrote a fine article on the question; his documentation and his conclusions are truly remarkable.[35] As he sees it, Kephas really means "Rock", and it is attributed to Peter. The play on words is quite

[29] J. Ringger, *op. cit.;* H. Clavier, "Petros kai petra," in *Studien für R. Bultmann* (Berlin, 1945), pp. 94-109; J. Betz, "Christus, Petra, Petrus," in *Kirche und Ueberlieferung: Festschrift J. R. Geiselmann* (Freiburg im Br., 1960), pp. 1-21.

[30] A. Dell, "Mt. 16, 17-19," in *Zeitschrift für neut. Wiss.* 15 (1914), pp. 1-49, on the authority of J. Wellhausen, *Das Evangelium Matthaei* (1904), p. 285, who admits, however, that the word is both masculine and feminine in Aramaean.

[31] Cf. J. Ringger, *op. cit.*, pp. 274-75.

[32] *Ibid.*, p. 275.

[33] See J. Ringger, *op. cit.*, nn. 12-61, 312-68; K. Schmidt, *Die Kirche*, p. 286; J. Jeremias, *Golgotha und die heilige Felsen* (Leipzig, 1926), p. 109, n. 6.

[34] E. Schweizer, *Das Leben des Herrn* (Zurich, 1946); *Idem, Gemeinde nach dem N.T.* (Zurich, ²1949), pp. 11ff.; A. Schlatter, *Matthaeuskommentar* (Stuttgart, 1929), p. 507. Others take the two meanings without deciding between them. J. Lagrange, *Evangile selon saint Matthieu* (*Etudes bibliques*) (Paris, 1948), p. 324.

[35] H. Clavier, *op. cit.*

natural in Aramaean, since "Rock" is used twice: "You are Rock
and on this Rock." By contrast, a change of gender was required in Greek, as in French.

The third question is not debated. "Kephas" and "Petros" are
not recognized names in the Judaic world, the Greek world or the
Latin world. It is the name of a thing. The name-change is a fact
attested to by history itself.

That Jesus did give this name to Simon is admitted by a large
number of exegetes, but there are exceptions, of course.[36] Without doubt, "Kephas" cannot be put on the same footing as
"Boanerges", which was applied to the sons of Zebedee (Mk. 3,
17). The latter epithet did not and could not have a future;
Matthew and Luke let it drop by the wayside. In the other case,
however, tradition has made a personal name out of a noun des-
ignating a thing. Paul picks it up without translating it; thus, in
his works, "Kephas" has supplanted "Simon". Paul uses "Peter"
only twice, in the second letter to the Galatians (Gal. 2, 7-8).

We cannot say with certainty when Jesus did confer this name
on Peter. No conclusion can be drawn from Mark 3, 16, Matthew 10, 2 and Luke 6, 14, which link the conferral of the name
to the institution of the college. One might say that Mark and
Luke add this note to distinguish Peter from another Simon (Mk.
3, 18; Lk. 6, 15). In the gospel of John, Jesus gives Peter the
name "Kephas" at their first meeting (1, 42), but this gospel
could well be alluding to a later event.[37]

In the light of the texts, one can conclude that the name
("Kephas" and "Petros") given to Simon as an epithet quickly
turned into a proper name. The translating of "Kephas" into
"Petros" testifies to the fact that the translator was aware that it

[36] E. Fascher, "Petrus," in *Pauly-Wissowa, Realencycl.* 19, 2 (1937), pp.
1355-61; W. Kuemmel, *Kirchenbegriff,* pp. 50-51; O. Cullmann, *Pierre,*
p. 26; G. Schulze-Kadelbach, "Die Stellung des Petrus in der Urgemeinde,"
in *Theol. Literat. Zeit.* 81 (1956), pp. 1-14; E. Dinkler, *Petrus,* p. 194;
H. Rheinfelden, "Philologische Erwägungen zu Mt 16, 18," in *Bibl.
Zeitschr.* 24 (1938), pp. 139-63 feels that the name "Kephas" was not
actually given to Simon by Christ but only promised.

[37] R. Schnackenburg, *Das Johannesevangelium* I (Freiburg im Br.,
1965), pp. 310-12.

was an epithet, for proper names were not translated. This is an important point, already recognized by K. Holl and emphasized by J. Schmidt.[38] We shall try to draw some conclusions from this fact later on.

O. Cullmann has constructed a picture of Peter's apostolate in which some older exegetical positions pave the way for his thesis.[39] Haenchen, the noted author of the best commentary on Acts, has gone over Cullmann's points with a fine tooth comb.[40] Let us try to set these two differing positions alongside each other.

Our image of the Petrine apostolate depends on the exegesis of Acts and Galatians 1—2. When he wrote Galatians, Paul had already gone up to Jerusalem twice and had met Peter there. It is difficult for us to know, says Haenchen, what the two apostles said to each other at their first meeting. We do know a little more about their second meeting but, as he notes, we only know it through Luke. The question is simple: Does Luke, as Cullmann claims, give us to understand that Peter has given up the direction of the Jerusalem Church in order to direct the Judaeo-Christian mission? Would this apostle have ceded his place to James after the persecution of 44 A.D. (Acts 12, 17)? It is fairly certain that Peter was involved in missionary activity in Samaria (Acts 8, 25), but, notes Haenchen, his trips to Lydia, Joppa and Caesarea were undertaken solely to found communities. In Acts 15 one finds no trace of a missionary apostolate. There is no justification for Cullmann's comment (on Acts 12, 9): "The author of Acts had only one intention in mind, to show Peter's definitive transition to an exclusively missionary activity." [41]

Cullmann finds support for this interpretation in 1 Corinthians 9, 5 where Paul speaks of other apostles, of the Lord's brothers, and of Cephas, who are accompanied by women in their travels.

---

[38] K. Holl, *Gesammelte Aufsätze zur Kirchengeschichte* II, p. 45; J. Schmidt, *Petrus der Fels*, pp. 355-59.

[39] O. Cullmann, *Pierre*, pp. 28-48.

[40] E. Haenchen, "Petrus-Probleme," in *New Test. Stud.* 7 (1960-61), pp. 187-197.

[41] O. Cullmann, *op. cit.*, p. 36.

He also finds support in Galatians 2, 9 where the three "pillars" —James, Kephas and John—are named in order according to the authority they exercise. As a missionary of Judaeo-Christianity, then, Peter would be under the direction of James and the Church at Jerusalem.

Haenchen notes that outside of Acts 8, 25 Luke never presents Peter as one engaging in missionary activity alone. When Cullmann claims that Peter came to the Council of Jerusalem not as the head of the Church but as "the representative of the mission directed by Jerusalem", Haenchen replies curtly: "On this matter Luke says nothing at all." [42] In fact, Luke does not even insinuate that this is the case. According to Haenchen, we get quite a different picture from Acts 15, 6-7; there Peter appears as the apostle who directs the community along with the elders and, as such, is named first (15, 22-23) as the author of the so-called apostolic decree.

After the death of Agrippa, Peter did not have to leave Jerusalem. In 1 Corinthians 9, 5 there is no question of missionary activity; the brothers of the Lord are mentioned, and Peter is mentioned last in a roll call that goes from lowest to highest—"The bishop comes last in a procession, not first," according to Haenchen. It is true that in Galatians 2, 9 Paul mentions James before Peter, but this is done only because the juxtaposition of James and John would have made one think of the sons of Zebedee. In this trilogy it would not be natural to distinguish James the bishop, John the apostle, and Peter the missionary. This text only shows that at that particular moment the Church of Jerusalem was rulled by these three men. Finally, says Haenchen, it is wrong to put Paul, the apostle of the Gentiles, on the same level as Peter, the apostle to the circumcised. Paul's reasoning had been false; he should have compared himself to James, Peter's true superior in Cullmann's view.

---

[42] *Ibid.* The German edition is more radical: "Acts 12, 17 simply points out that Peter's release marks his entry into full-time, exclusive missionary work, the task for which he had been gradually preparing himself" (*Petrus,* p. 45).

It is evident, then, that the views of Cullmann and Haenchen differ, and that Cullmann's interpretation seems to go beyond the text and to be somewhat faulty.[43]

We should like to mention briefly the studies of G. Klein; they demonstrate the keenness of their author, have a full bibliography, and contain some astonishing conclusions.[44] Klein sets out to depict three stages in the life of Peter: Peter among the Twelve, the apostle of Jerusalem, and Peter as a colonist without the preeminence of authority that a later view developed. The scenes depicting Peter's denial are not historical. Luke rehabilitated Peter. Here history is being written upside down, in conformity with the legendary crucifixion of Peter!

Finally, let us mention a few critics who refuse to admit Peter's death at Rome. K. Heussi has written several studies, trying to prove that Peter died before 56 A.D.[45] He bases his conclusion on Galatians 2, 9 where the verb "ēsan" would seem to refer to a situation that no longer exists. This is also the position of two Americans: D. F. Robinson and C. M. Smaltz;[46] the latter settles on 44 A.D. as the date of Peter's death, in prison. J. Munck pur-

[43] A fine reconstruction of Peter's last years has been given by Ch. Nesbitt, "What Did Become of Peter?" in *Journ. Bibl. Lit.* (1959), pp. 10-16.

[44] G. Klein, "Galater 2, 6-9 und die Geschichte der Jerusalem Urgemeinde," in *Zeitschr. für Theol. Kirche* 57 (1960), pp. 275-95; *Idem*, "Die Verleugnung des Petrus," *ibid.*, 58 (1961), pp. 285-328.

[45] See especially *Die römische Petrustradition in kritischer Sicht* (Tübingen, 1955). The other productions of the same author are cited by E. Dinkler, "Die Petrus-Rom Frage: Eine Forschungsbericht," in *Theol. Rundschau* 25 (1959), p. 193. Dinkler presents all the comments that have been made on Heussi's positions. The thesis has been severely criticized by many exegetes. Cf. E. Dinkler, *Petrus*, pp. 199-202; O. Cullmann, *Petrus*, p. 85; K. Aland, "Wann starb Petrus? Eine Bemerkung zu Gal 2,6," in *N.T. Stud.* 2 (1956), pp. 265-75; E. Burton, *The Epistle to the Galatians* (Edinburgh, ⁵1956), pp. 87-88.

[46] D. Robinson, "Where and When Did Peter Die?" in *Journ. Bibl. Lit.* 64 (1945), pp. 255-67; C. Smaltz, "Did Peter Die in Jerusalem?", *ibid.*, 71 (1952), pp. 211-16. See also H. Katzenmager, "Die Schicksale des Petrus von seinem Aufenthalt in Korinth bis seinem Martyrertod," in *Intern. Kirch. Zeitschr.* 34 (1944), pp. 145-52. We shall not discuss the question of the Vatican excavations: see Dinkler, *Petrus*, pp. 189-230, 289-335; 27 (1961), pp. 33-64. We should also mention the fine studies

ports to find the first testimony to the death of Peter and Paul in Rome in Apocalypse 11, 3-13.[47]

But we have spent enough time on the major points of controversy over Peter's biography. Let us now tackle Matthew 16, 18 in earnest.

2. *Peter's Primacy*

The exegetes are unanimous in associating Peter's primacy with three Gospel texts: Matthew 16, 16-18; Luke 22, 31-32; John 21, 1-14. Of these three texts, the first is by far the most important and most crucial.[48] It is this text that we shall focus on here. To give a clear presentation of the problem, we shall start with the literary questions and then move on to the historical and doctrinal conclusions.

(a) *Literary Problems.* The Matthaean text (Mt. 16, 13-23) follows Mark in verses 13 to 16, and falls in line with Mark again in verses 20-23; in verses 20-23 there are a few slight differences between the two gospels, but they do not make them significantly different. Verses 17 to 19 are peculiar to Matthew. Verse 17 is a blessing reserved for Simon, the son of Jona, who had declared: "You are the Christ, the Son of God." This declaration was not something he had learned from flesh and blood; it was something revealed to him by the heavenly Father. Verse 18 contains two statements by Jesus: "You are Peter, and upon this Rock I will build my Church, and the gates of hell shall not prevail against her." Verse 19 talks about the granting of the keys to Peter, the right to bind and loose on earth.

It is impossible to deny the Semitic character of the passage:

---

of J. Ruyschaert, "Réflections sur les fouilles vaticanes," in *Rev. Hist. Eccles.* 48 (1953), pp. 573-638; 49 (1954), pp. 5-58; also cf. by the same author *Recherches et études autour de la Confession de la Basilique Vaticane (1940-58): Etat de la question et Bibliographie.* (Vatican, 1958), pp. 3-47. See also O. Cullmann, *Petrus,* pp. 148-78, in which the bibliography up to 1960 has been utilized.

[47] J. Munck, *Petrus und Paulus in der Offenbarung Johannis* (Copenhagen, 1950).

[48] This point is recognized by many Protestant authors.

(1) Simon Bar-Jona; (2) flesh and blood; (3) revealed; (4) heavenly Father; (5) Peter-Kephas; (6) the gates of hell or Sheol; (7) the keys; (8) the kingdom of heaven; (9) bind and loose. Here we shall not discuss "heavenly Father" and "kingdom of heaven" because they are typical Matthaean expressions.[49]

"Bar Jona", which is rendered "son of John" in the gospel of St. John (1, 42), has been interpreted by R. Eisler as meaning "anarchist, revolutionary, member of the extremist anti-Roman faction".[50] In the Bible "flesh and blood" represents the weak element in man (Sir. 14, 18; 1 Cor. 15, 50; Gal. 1, 16; Eph. 6, 12; Heb. 2, 14). "Kephas" and "the gates of sheol" are positively identified. In the Old Testament, the "key" confers a power based on a teaching (Is. 22, 22). Let us stress the word "revelation", which plays a large role in the Qumran texts. To this list one can add the word "Church", to designate the messianic community. The vocabulary of the Essenes leaves no room for doubt. Several important studies have highlighted this fact.[51]

With the Semitic character of the passage definitely established, we can now consider the question of its *origin*. No one today regards the pericope (16, 17-20) as a late interpolation into Matthew's text.[52] Once upon a time some claimed, without good reason, that this addition was of Roman origin. A more serious challenge is the view which attributes these verses to a primitive community. The opinions are many and varied. Some thought of a community where Aramaean was the vernacular, of a Syrian community, and more precisely of the community at Antioch.[53]

[49] Cf. J. Jeremias, *Theol. Wörterbuch. z. N.T.* 3, p. 410; J. Schmid, *Lex. Theol. und Kirche* 5, p. 1113; R. Schnackenburg, *Johannesevangelium* (Freiburg im Br., 1965), p. 311.

[50] R. Eisler, *Jesus Basileus* (Heidelberg, 1929), pp. 67ff.; J. Jeremias, *Theol. Wörterb. z. N.T.* 3, pp. 743ff.

[51] See, for example, B. Reicke, "Die Verfassung der Urgemeinde im Lichte jüd. Dokumente," in *Theologische Zeitschrift* 10 (1954), pp. 95-112; H. Kosmala, *Hebräer-Essener-Christen* (Leiden, 1959).

[52] See F.-M. Braun, *Neues Licht,* pp. 76-81.

[53] The Aramaean base is admitted by R. Bultmann, *Geschichte des synopt. Tradition* (Göttingen, ²1931), p. 147; W. Kuemmel, *Kirchenbegriff,* p. 20; O. Cullmann, "Petros," in *Theol. Wörterb. z. N.T.* 6 (1955),

In the first case, the primitive Jerusalem Church would be the best bet; as a matter of fact, the Semitic cast of the vocabulary argues for this interpretation. However, exegetical criticism was not content with this view. Some critics deny that these words have any connection with the historical Jesus;[54] others grant some connection, but the number of words attributed to Jesus himself varies from author to author.[55]

The "form-criticism" school tries to explain the genesis of the pericope. Some exegetes of this school feel that one must start with the conferral of the name "Kephas" to Peter, the foundation on which the "legend" of the conferral of the primacy and the keys developed.[56] For Stauffer, Matthew uses these verses to sum up the general position that Peter held in tradition, and to exalt him as the one who received the first vision of Jesus after his resurrection.[57] H. Lehmann supports this viewpoint, and he regards Matthew 16, 13-20 as an indirect paschal story.[58] Vögtle's studies, cited previously, have tackled this question in authoritative fashion.[59] R. Bultmann subscribes to the thesis of Lehmann,[60] while Hirsch rounds it out by adding that the conferral of a new name was integrated into this vision story. In these

---

pp. 105-06; origins at Antioch proposed by H. Strathmann, "Die Stellung des Petrus in der Urkirche: Zur Frühgeschichte des Wortes an Petrus, Mt 16, 17-19," in *Zeitschr. für syst. Theol.* 20 (1943), pp. 223-83. H. von Campenhausen sees it as being somewhere other than Jerusalem: *Kirchliches Amt und geistliche Vollmacht* (Tübingen, 1953), p. 142. See also J. Klink, *Het Petrustype in het Nieuwe Testament en de Oudchristelijke Letterkunde* (Leiden, 1947).

[54] This position ties in with the problem of Jesus and the Church discussed earlier. See A. Oepke, *op. cit.*

[55] The blessing of Peter is accepted, but not the verses on the primacy.

[56] Especially E. Stauffer, "Zur Vor- und Frühgeschichte des Primatus Petri," in *Zeitschr. f. Kirchengeschichte* 62 (1943-44), pp. 1-34, esp. p. 24.

[57] E. Stauffer, *op. cit.*, p. 25.

[58] H. Lehmann, "Du bist Petrus: Zum Problem von Matthäus 16, 13-26," in *Evang. Theol.* 13 (1953), p. 60.

[59] See above, pp. 153f.

[60] R. Bultmann, Die frage nach dem messianischen Bewusstsein Jesu und das Petrusbekenntnis," in *Zeitschr. f. neut. Wiss.* 19 (1919-20), p. 173; *Idem, Theologie des N.T.* (Tübingen, 1948), p. 46; less definite in *Das Evangelium nach Johannes* (Göttingen, ¹³1953, pp. 551-52.

verses the Church has expressed her awareness of an absolute authority.[61]

In short, the present-day exegetical positions are quite distinct from one another. Some say it is impossible to get back to the words of Jesus. Others say that the ancient, Semitic cast of the *logion* favors an authentic origin. There is no doubt that here the confessional allegiance of the exegete comes into play. Catholic exegetes do not deny that there are signs of Matthew's editing in Matthew 16, 13-23. They also admit that verses 17-20 are additions of the first gospel to an earlier strand of words represented in Mark.[62] They also realize that the earlier traditions could have acquired new shape and borrowed outside vocabulary within the primitive Church.

The correspondence between the words of Jesus and their redaction within the Church and the gospel of Matthew is a question which goes beyond this one pericope. The exegete's view on the authenticity of the words themselves plays a large role in his outlook. The exegete who attributes priority to Jesus —at least insofar as there is no sure evidence of actual creation by the community or the editor—finds himself in a different position than the critic who takes an *a priori* position in favor of the community, going back to Jesus only when he finds it impossible to explain a passage or an event without him.

In the present case, we shall follow A. Vögtle[63] and try to analyze the pericope as exactly as possible. We can distinguish the "blessing" genre in verse 17, which fits in well with the utilization of this genre in Jesus' preaching. Verses 18-19 rest on solid ground: the name change; the correspondence of the traditions represented here with the overall Synoptic traditions; the role of Peter as the foundation of unity and stability in the community of disciples. There is no question of a juridical demonstra-

---

[61] E. Hirsch, *Frügeschichte des Evangeliums* II (Tübingen, 1941), pp. 306-07.

[62] J. Schmid, *Das Evangelium nach Matthäus* (Regensburg, [8]1956).

[63] A. Vögtle, "Messiasbekenntnis und Petrusverleugnung," in *Bibl. Zeitschr.* 1 (1957), pp. 252-72; 2 (1958), pp. 85-103. On the order of priority of the Matthaean sources, see Obrist, *op. cit.*, pp. 59-60.

tion here; the text cannot be put on formal trial. On varying levels it bears witness to a living tradition that has come down to us through Matthew's hands.

A final question arises. Does Matthew put this logion in the best place? Even if one admits that it has direct or remote origins in Jesus, isn't another solution possible? A certain number of exegetes find it more prudent to avoid all guesswork.[64] This is not the case with others. E. Stauffer, who does not grant any relationship between the historical Jesus and the risen Christ, classes Matthew 16, 17 among the authoritative words of the Risen One.[65] On the other hand, others connect it with the story of the passion, and Peter's betrayal in particular.[66] R. Lichtenhan regards these verses as the contrary to Luke 22, 31. For Cullmann, who admits the historicity of the texts, they fit in with the allusion of John 21, 15-19; more precisely, the text is a logical followup to Luke 22, 31-34.[67] Jesus would have pronounced these words after he predicted Peter's denial to be "a great exegetical probability", to which Cullmann is especially attracted. But the arguments in favor of this hypothesis make it no more than an acceptable possibility.[68]

Several authors have attacked this reconstruction, maintaining Matthew's positioning of these verses does not lack reasonable-

---

[64] K. Schmidt, *Die Kirche des Urchristentums*, p. 283; W. Kümmel, *Geschichtsbewusstsein*, p. 21; R. Rohren, *Das Problem der Kirchenzucht im N.T.*, (Zurich, 1952), p. 31.

[65] E. Stauffer, *Zur Vor-und Frühgeschichte*, p. 29.

[66] R. Lichtenhan, *Die urchristliche Mission* (Bâle, 1946), pp. 9-10.

[67] O. Cullmann, *Pierre*, pp. 207-14; see the complementary article by Cullmann, "L'apôtre Pierre, instrument du Diable et instrument de Dieu," in *New Testament Essays for T.M. Manson* (Manchester, 1959), pp. 94-105.

[68] On the Catholic side, cf. J. Schmid, *Das Evangelium nach Matthäus*, p. 245; M. Boismard, *Divus Thomas* 31 (Fribourg, 1953), p. 326; P. Benoit, *Rev. bibl.* 60 (1953), p. 571; *Idem*, "La primauté de saint Pierre selon le N.T." in *Istina* 18 (1955), pp. 318-19; above all, A. Vögtle, "Des Petrus die Verheissung und Erfüllung," in *Münch. Theol. Zeitschr.* 5 (1954), p. 15; *Idem*, "Messiasbekenntnis und Petrusverheissung," *Bibl. Zeitschr.* 1 (1957), pp. 253-72; 2 (1958), pp. 85-103, shifting the pericope. On Cullmann's overall position, see J. Frisque, *Oscar Cullmann: Une théologie de l'histoire du salut* (Tournai, 1960).

ness, or that Jesus could have spoken them more than once.[69] To study every exegetical variation would carry us too far. Looking at it objectively, we can say that it is difficult to come to a definitive judgment. Their positioning by Matthew and their positioning by various exegetes cannot be accepted with full reliability.

(b) *Historical and Doctrinal Problems.* The historical and doctrinal problems raised by Matthew 16, 18-19 can be grouped under these four themes: (1) Simon is called Rock; (2) the establishment and the stability of the Church; (3) the conferral of the keys; (4) the powers of Peter. After studying these four themes, we shall try to set forth the question of succession.

(1) Assuming that the exegete accepts the notion that the historical Jesus did in fact call Peter "Rock", he finds himself attracted to one of two basic choices. Protestants used to interpret "Rock" as referring not to the person of Peter but to his faith; this position is now outdated. It is condemned by many Protestant exegetes who criticize Luther's interpretation on philological grounds.[70] But traces of this dogmatic position are still retained in certain interpretations; they admit that Peter is the Rock, but only because of his messianic confession.[71]

By this very fact, then, all notions of succession are eliminated; it is the admission of Jesus' messianism that becomes the rock of the Church, and all the faithful share in it. Some exegetes, however, realize that this explanation is forced; it does not account for the logion in its totality and it contradicts John 21, 15-17.[72]

Some Catholics focus on the connection between Peter's confession and the designation as "Rock", concluding that "because Peter was blessed with this divine light, Jesus proclaims him

[69] F.-M. Braun, review of Cullmann, in *Rev. Thomiste* 53 (1953), p. 397; M. Meinertz, *Zeitschr. f. Miss. und Wiss.* (1953), p. 238. Braun challenges the conclusions which Cullmann draws from the transposition.

[70] See F. Obrist, *Echtheitsfragen,* pp. 79-87; cf. A. Argyle, *The Gospel according to Matthew* (The Cambridge Bible Commentary) (Cambridge, 1963): "Even if it refers to Peter, it refers to him as the spokesman of this faith" (p. 116).

[71] H. Clavier, *Petros kai petra,* p. 107.

[72] O. Cullmann, *art. cit.,* "Petros," p. 98.

blessed (compare Mt. 13, 16ff.) and gives him primacy in his Church—a primacy that is primarily of a doctrinal character".[73] T. Gallus goes even further, regarding it as the foundation of infallibility.[74] This theological deduction does not seem to us to be inherent in the text itself.

Even if Peter is the Rock, he can be so in different ways. First of all, we might consider him as the first foundation for the start of the Church. This chronological explanation is maintained by Th. Zahn, G. Wehrung, J. Horst and H. Strathmann.[75] It is based on Paul's assertion that Christ is the only foundation of the Church (1 Cor. 3, 11), and on the distinction between the foundation (the apostles) and the cornerstone (Jesus) in Ephesians 2, 20. It is clear that the contexts and the doctrines are different. Peter is the Rock only through Jesus, and the Lord remains the true author of the Church.

The second explanation for "Rock" paves the way for a positive exegesis. Since the Church is the continuation of the work of Jesus, Peter can assume a basic position in that Church; he is the Rock on which the community is built.[76] For some exegetes, Peter is the symbol, the type of the true believer, through his confession.[77] For others, the larger number in fact, Peter received a promise that is fulfilled at a later stage in his apostolic career.[78] Peter is the apostle-rock for the foundation of the Church, not for her maintenance. This is the well-known position of Oscar Cullmann.[79] Many reviews of Cullmann's books have

[73] P. Benoit, "Saint Pierre d'après Cullmann," in *Exégèse et Théologie* II (Paris, 1961), p. 302.

[74] T. Gallus, "Primatus infallibilitatis in metaphora 'Petra' indicatus," in *Verbum Domini* 30 (1952), pp. 193-204; *Idem*, "De primatu infallibilitatis ex Mt 16, 13-18 eruendo," *ibid.*, 33 (1955), pp. 209-14.

[75] Th. Zahn, *Matthäus* (Leipzig, '1922), p. 540; G. Wehrung, *Kirche nach evangelischen Verständnis* (Gütersloh, 1947); J. Horst, "Der Kirchengedanke bei Matthäus," in *Zeitschr. f. syst. Theol.* 20 (1943), pp. 127-45.

[76] This question is linked to teachings about the visible and invisible Church, the Church in heaven and the Church on earth.

[77] See R. Bultmann, *Die Frage*, p. 143.

[78] J. Leenhardt, *Etudes sur l'Eglise dans le N.T.* (Geneva, 1940), pp. 28-29.

[79] O. Cullmann, *Pierre*, pp. 193-200.

rejected this thesis. Cerfaux writes: "It is true that Peter is the first stone placed on the foundation of the Church, the stone which will support the others. Chronologically, the act of founding will never be repeated, and takes place once for all time." [80] But Matthew 16, 18-19 is not to be regarded as a comment on the positioning of the Rock alone, but rather a comment on the ongoing situation of the Rock, the existence and the function of the foundation. R. Baumann, the Protestant exegete, has acknowledged the communitarian character of the "foundation" and of a necessary and durable "foundation".[81] His position caused him to incur a condemnation from a special session of the Wurtemberg *Landeskirche* in 1953.[82] A. Vögtle considers Cullmann's position to be wrong.[83]

A third explanation of "Rock" brings up another complex of exegetical problems. It starts out from the utilization of the "stone" theme in the Old Testament. It relies particularly on Isaiah 28, 14-19 for Matthew 16, 18ff., and on Zechariah 3, 1-9 for Luke 22, 31-32.[84] To this basic source of inspiration it adds some parallels from Jewish rabbinism. Abraham and the patriarchs form the foundation for the construction of the chosen people. It is in this perspective that the studies of J. Jeremias and H. Schmidt, which were utilized and developed by J. Ringger, acquire their true value.[85] We are dealing with mythical and symbolic language, where the stones support the Holy of Holies at Jerusalem. Finally, the Qumran texts reveal that the "Rock" image was alive in the Jewish mentality during Christ's time on earth. The studies of O. Betz[86] highlight many passages where

[80] L. Cerfaux, "Saint Pierre et sa succession," in *Ephem. Theol. Lov.* 29 (1953), p. 189.

[81] R. Baumann, *Der Petrus Bekenntnis und Schlüssel* (Stuttgart, 1950).

[82] See F. Obrist, *Echtheitsfragen,* p. 110. Against Baumann, see Cullmann, *Pierre,* p. 200, n. 3.

[83] A. Vögtle, *Der Petrus,* pp. 18-19.

[84] J. Klink, *Het Petrustype* (Leiden, 1947); P. Dreyfus, "La primauté de Pierre à la lumière de la théologie biblique du reste d'Israël," in *Istina* 2 (1955), pp. 338-46; F. Refoulé, "Primauté de Pierre dans les Évangiles," in *Recherches Sc. relig.* 38 (1964), pp. 1-41.

[85] J. Jeremias, *Golgotha und der Hl. Fels* (Leipzig, 1926); H. Schmidt, *Der Heilige Fels in Jerusalem* (Tübingen, 1933); J. Ringger, *op. cit.*

[86] O. Betz, "Felsenmann und Felsengemeinde: Eine Parallele zu Mt 16,

the eschatological community is pictured as being founded on rock, in opposition to the forces of the subterranean world. Thus we get a picture of Peter preserving his place and his rock-function as the base and the support of the edifice, the Church.

Now this does not mean that the Protestant view agrees with the Catholic interpretation. In the Protestant view, Peter remains as the foundation through his word, his enduring testimony that is found in the New Testament writings. Benoit has criticized this position, for the simple reason that the first Christians never regarded the apostles "as having solely the function of writers".[87]

However, there are some Protestant theologians who do reconcile themselves with Catholic teaching to some extent.[88] While condemning the primacy as it is exercised by Rome, they do acknowledge that the Church necessarily requires ministers and that the existence of a doctrinal and pastoral authority is in line with Christ's wishes.

(2) Insofar as the establishment of the Church and her stability is concerned, we may say that verses 18b and 19a form one unit. The first initiates the construction of the Church. It should be noted that Christ keeps the initiative here and that it is an eschatological activity. The time span involved is not within the earthly time span of Jesus. Some see a purely eschatological intention in this passage,[89] while others see a period immediately following Christ's death and resurrection[90] or one which combines

---

17-19 in den Qumrânpsalmen," in *Zeitschr. f. neut. Wiss.* 48 (1957), pp. 49-77.

[87] P. Benoit, *op. cit.,* p. 299. The whole problem of "sola Scriptura" crops up here and becomes the focal point of the argument. Starting from this point, Catholics develop the argument along historical lines. They say that it is a matter of historical fact that, however privileged the New Testament scriptures may be, the New Testament teaching on the living reality of the new covenant goes beyond what is contained in these scriptures. Just as every attempt at exegesis goes beyond the written text, so the written text does not go to the depth of their authors' actual situation. Life and Scripture shed light on each other.

[88] This is not only the case with Baumann, but with all the Eastern and Western Churches that acknowledge episcopal authority by ordination and the legitimacy of apostolic succession.

[89] See E. Lohmeyer, *Die Grundlagen der paulinischen Eschatologie* (Tübingen, 1929), p. 158.

[90] Ph. Vilhauer, *Oikodomè: Das Bild vom Bau in der christlichen*

resurrection and parousia within the same perspective.[91] In
Matthew's terminology, the Church is neither the group of Jesus'
apostles nor the final kingdom (because of 19a), but the messianic community. The longed-for Messiah is always united to
a community. Throughout the New Testament this theme of
building is to be found. The community is identified with the
temple, the house, the process of building. Christ constructs a
temple that is not made by human hands (1 Pet. 2, 5). This
Church is not a dead edifice; she is a living complex. Ephesians
2, 19-21 tells us that she is an edifice built on the foundation
of the apostles and prophets, with Christ as the chief cornerstone,
and that she will be fitted together and grow into a holy temple.
In Matthew there is no doubt that Peter occupies a choice position
in this definite, ongoing eschatological process of construction.

Once upon a time the term "gates of hell" was explained as
the personification of the forces of the kingdom of the dead which
imprisoned all who descended there.[92] Since the studies of
J. Jeremias have come out, another strand of symbolism has been
added to the phrase. Hell would be the place of punishment where
the impious await judgment. The gates of hell, then, symbolize
the hellish powers of Satan and the evil spirits who rise to attack
the Church.[93] E. Eppel sees a Semitic substrate and would prefer
to read "gate-keepers" instead of "gates"; this would strengthen
Jeremias' interpretation, which is already admitted.[94]

The Jerusalem Bible has this commentary: the gates of hell
"personify the forces of evil which enslave man in the death of
sin and then finally bind him in eternal death forever". The two
explanations are thus intermingled and given a theological cast.

The Qumran texts shed new light on the expression. A fragment from the Testament of Levi (2, 3-5), published by Milik
and cited by Allegro, situates the holy mountain connecting

Literatur von N.T. bis Clemens Alexandrinus (Heidelberg, 1940), p. 14.
[91] O. Michel, *Theol. Wörterb.z. N.T.* 5 (1955), p. 141.
[92] O. Cullmann, *Pierre,* p. 183.
[93] J. Jeremias, *Golgotha,* p. 110; *Idem,* "Adēs," in *Theol. Wörterb. z. N.T.* 1, p. 655.
[94] E. Eppel, "L'interprétation de Matthieu 16, 18," in *Mélanges Goguel* (Neuchâtel, 1950), pp. 71-73.

heaven and earth at the foot of Hermon, so that Galilee could be linked up with Jewish apocalyptic notions. The word "Kepha" is presented by Milik to fill up a gap; it is a word which appears in another Aramaean fragment belonging to the 89th chapter of the Book of Henoch. There it is Moses who receives his revelation on the Rock. Likewise, in the Qumran Hymns (Ps. 6), we read: "You set the foundation on the rock." This could be translated, says Carmignac, as: "You set the committee (= my community) on the rock." [95]

(3) Apropos of verse 19 and the conferral of the keys, Cullmann poses a preliminary question. He feels that between the "rock" theme and this verse there is very little connection.[96] Being the rock is the trait of an apostle, while the power of the keys could be transmitted to a non-apostolic authority. This opinion is not shared by many exegetes, who see Matthew 16, 19 as a development of 16, 18.[97] This verse spells out the "rock" image. There are no divergent explanations regarding the unity between the keys and the power of binding and loosing.

What does the power of the keys signify? The Protestant critics who interpret verse 19 as a later creation of the community find no difficulty in regarding it as an expression of the totality of powers.[98] These powers are exercised on earth, because the promised keys are not the keys of heaven but the keys which give entrance into the kingdom of God. The explanation provided by the verse is very clear. Peter is not only the Rock on which Christ builds his Church; he also exercises a supernatural authority.

[95] J. Allegro, *The Dead Sea Scrolls* (London, 1956), pp. 142-44; J. Carmignac, *Les textes de Qumran traduits et annotés* (Paris, 1961), p. 224.

[96] O. Cullmann, *Pierre*, p. 190.

[97] Whatever the ultimate sources of the logion may be, the conclusion holds true in terms of the final composition.

[98] Many authors, even those in the critical camp, admit unreservedly that the formula involves the power of teaching and of directing. These exegetes regard this verse as a creation of the primitive community and hence attribute full meaning to the words. Among these exegetes are: R. Bultmann, *Geschichte*, p. 147; W. Kümmel, *Geschichtsbewusstsein*, pp. 22, 41; E. Stauffer, *Zur Vor- und Frühgeschichte*, pp. 25, 61; Strathmann, *Die Stellung*, p. 269; H. von Campenhausen, *Kirchliches Amt*, pp. 141-42.

The object of this authority can have reference to teaching and providing direction in the Church. For the Protestant exegete, teaching consists in preaching the Word of God and confessing the faith, which Peter will have to go on doing after Jesus has disappeared.[99] Sometimes the exegetes state specifically that this authority should be related to the preaching of the risen Jesus and that it should be restricted to the apostles' testimony to this fact.[100]

Others see the conferral of the keys as a mission to uncover the meaning of the Old Testament writings.[101] The Pharisees and the scribes are dispossessed of the authority which they exercised so badly, and it redounds to the benefit of Peter and the apostles.

Some Catholics claim that the power of the keys has much wider scope.[102] It is not just a question of doctrine alone, but of the whole salvation economy. The symbolism of the keys seems to them to include the power of administration and of commandment. When it is given to Peter, it places him in a privileged position of authority; by the very nature of the privilege, his power of the keys is limited only by the duration of the Church herself.[103] The universal character of the power granted by the conferral of the keys is not admitted by J. Jeremias.[104]

(4) The formula "binding and loosing", which is related to

---

[99] W. Vischer, *Der evangelische Gemeindeordnung: Mt 16, 19-20, 18 ausgelegt* (Zurich, 1951), p. 24.

[100] O. Cullmann, *Pierre*, p. 184.

[101] G. Wehrung, *Kirche*, pp. 178-79; F. Kattenbusch, *Der Spruch über Petrus*, pp. 120-21; K. Goetz, *Petrus als Gründer und Oberhaupt der Kirche und Schauer von Gesichten nach den altchristlichen Berichten und legenden* (Untersuch z. N.T., 13) (Leipzig, 1927).

[102] The direct power of teaching is proposed by K. Adam, "Aum ausserkanonischen und kanonischen Sprachgebrauch von Binden und Lösen," in *Theol. Quartalschr.* 96 (1914), pp. 49-64, 161-197; J. Geiselmann, "Der Perinische Primat (Mt 16, 17), seine neueste Bekämpfung und Rechfertigung," in *Bibl. Zeitfragen* 12/7 (1927), pp. 217-224.

[103] See A. Vögtle, *Des Petrus der Verheissung*, p. 34; P. Benoit, *op. cit.*, p. 302: "Peter is appointed by Jesus as the 'prime minister' of his Church; he will have to govern not only the masses of the faithful but the officers themselves as well."

[104] J. Jeremias, "Kleis," in *Theol. Wörterbuch z. N.T.* 3 (1938), pp. 749-53, restricts the power of the keys to the power of preaching, because of Matthew 23, 13.

rabbinic terminology, is disputed as far as its meaning is concerned. Some point out the parallel between John 20, 23 and Matthew 16, 19; in the former, this power is applied to the apostles and disciples, so it should be regarded as the property of the community. Peter is only the representative of this community.[105]

Others admit that Peter's privileged position must be recognized, and they give the formula a meaning that is close to that of Catholic doctrine. If one restricts its meaning to the power of settling disputes and conflicts—as rabbis did—one does not seem to have captured the full richness of the expression. Moreover, rabbinic authority involved not only the imposition of certain laws (*halachas*) but also the disciplinary practice of the community.[106] Stendhal sees an application of the first function in Matthew 16, 19, and the exercise of the second function in Matthew 18, 18.[107] This may be true. But it is a mistake to limit Peter's role to that of a rabbi, just as it is a mistake to limit his function to that of handing down judgments of expulsion. The gospel text makes clear that "binding and loosing" on earth has a counterpart in heaven.

Oscar Cullman is right in saying that "what Peter does for the *ekklesia* is efficacious for the kingdom of heaven which is to come".[108] Thus the scope of the text goes beyond a simple process of terrestrial judgment; it involves a supernatural value which finds expression in the forgiveness of sins. On this question, too, it is less a question of impartial textual exegesis and more a question of a confrontation between differing theological positions regarding the primacy and its mission. Any exegesis of the

[105] O. Cullmann, *Pierre,* p. 185; J. Jeremias, *op. cit.,* p. 751; R. Bultmann, *Geschichte,* p. 151; J. Klink, *Het Petrustype,* p. 122.

[106] H. Wendland, *Die Eschatologie des Reiches Gottes bei Jesus* (Gütersloh, 1931), p. 180. Some also attach to the community the power of binding and loosening: E. Schweizer, *Das Leben des Herrn in der Gemeinde und ihren Diensten* (Zürich, 1936), p. 93.

[107] K. Stendhal, *Matthew* (Peake's Commentary on the Bible) (London 1962), pp. 787-88, which is connected with Cullmann's ideas on the uniqueness of the Petrine privilege.

[108] O. Cullmann, *Pierre,* p. 184.

power of the keys and of "binding and loosing" depends on the exegesis of Peter the Rock, the foundation for the establishment of the Church.

By way of conclusion, let us quote the judicious remarks of F. Refoulé on the transmittability of Peter's prerogatives. As everyone knows, this question is a central preoccupation for Oscar Cullmann and many other exegetes and theologians. Refoulé remarks: The gospel texts, by themselves, do not explicitly affirm or rule out the possibility of such a transmission. In reality exegetes and theologians accept or reject this possibility on the basis of a certain conception of the Church and of the grace of the new covenant in comparison with the old. Differing theological syntheses thus confront one another, and that is why the debate has so far borne so little fruit.[109]

There is no doubt that on some important points Protestant exegesis has abandoned positions that were regarded as true for a long time by their camp. Catholic exegetes have made some attempts to avoid imposing on the texts a tone and a meaning that are nothing more than theological deductions. Only time will tell whether common love for truth and common respect for strict rules of objective interpretation will get the better of confessional disputes.

[109] F. Refoulé, "Primauté de Pierre dans les Évangiles" in *Recherches Sc. Rel.* 38 (1964), p. 39.

BIOGRAPHICAL NOTES

ADRIAN SHERWIN-WHITE: Born in Brentford, England, on August 10, 1911, this Anglican is a fellow of the British Academy, and a reader in ancient history at the University of Oxford, where he gained his doctorate in this subject. Among his publications are *Roman Society and Roman Law in the New Testament* (Oxford, 1963) and *Racial Prejudice in the Roman Empire* (Cambridge, 1967).

JAN-MARIA SZYMUSIAK, S.J.: Born in Germany on November 27, 1920, he was ordained in 1950. After studying at the University of Paris and at the Gregorian, Rome, he received doctorates in theology and letters. Since 1958 he has been professor of theological methodology and patrology in the Jesuit House of Studies in Warsaw, and of the history of Christian thought at the Catholic University of Lublin. He edits a Polish edition of patristic texts, and among his published works are *Eléments de théologie de l'homme selon Grégoire de Nazianze* (Rome, 1963) and *Grzegorz Teolog* (Poznan-Warsaw, 1965). He also contributes to *Recherches de Science Religieuse* (Paris), *Znak* (Cracow), etc.

ANTON WEILER: Born in the Netherlands on November 6, 1927, he gained his doctorate in letters in 1962 after studying at the Berchmanianum in Nijmegen and the Catholic University of Nijmegen. Since 1964 he has held professorships at Nijmegen University for medieval history, paleography and diplomatics, and since 1965 he has also lectured there on the philosophy of history. Among his published works are *Heinrich von Gorkum, Seine Stellung in der Philosophie und der Theologie des Spätmittelalters* (Hilversum, 1962) and *Nicolaas van Cues en de oecumenische problematiek vóór de Reformatie* (Bois-le-Duc, 1964). He is a well-known contributor to *Cahiers de civilisation médiévale* (Poitiers).

ADEL-THÉODORE KHOURY: Born in Lebanon on March 26, 1930, he is a Catholic of the Melkite rite. He was ordained in 1953, studying at the École Supérieure and the Oriental Institute in Beirut, and at the University of Lyons. He gained doctorates in philosophy, literature and Arabic studies in 1966, and is currently dean of studies at Münster University, where he has lectured on the science of religion since 1964.

Among his works are *Les Théologiens byzantins et l'Islam* (2 vols.) (Münster, 1966) and *Manuel II Paléologue: Entretiens avec un musulman* (Paris, 1966). He is a contributor to *Zeitschrift für Missionwissenschaft und Religionswissenschaft* (Münster) and *Proche-Orient Chrétien* (Jerusalem).

REINERUS POST: Born in Holland on May 18, 1894, he was ordained in 1919. He has been apostolic protonotary since 1959. He studied at the Rijsenburg Seminary and University of Utrecht, gaining his doctorate in history *cum laude* in 1928. He is professor emeritus at the University of Nijmegen, where he lectured on Church history and medieval history from 1937 to 1962. Among his published works are *Rapports ecclésiaux au Pays-Bas avant la Réforme de 1500 environ à environ 1580* (Utrecht, 1954) and *Histoire de l'Eglise des Pays-Bas au Moyen-Age* (2 vols.) (Utrecht, 1957). He is editor of the review *Archief voor de geschiedenis van de katholieke Kerk in Nederland.*

HENRI BERNARD-MAÎTRE, S.J.: Born in France on October 21, 1889, he was ordained in 1919. After studying at the École des Hautes Études in Tientsin, the Catholic Institute in Paris, and the Gregorian in Rome, he received his doctorate in mathematics in 1912. He has been a missionary in China, and from 1947–1963 he lectured at the Institute of Ethnology and Religious Sociology in Rome. Among his works are *Sagesse chinoise et Philosophie chrétienne* (1939) and *Les Humanités d'Extrême-Orient* (Cathasia): he is also a well-known contributor to *Monumenta Serica* and *Monumenta Nipponica.*

GEORG SCHWAIGER: Born in Germany on January 23, 1925, he was ordained in 1951. He studied at the University of Munich, gaining a doctorate in theology in 1950. He has been professor of Church history there since 1962. He has published *Die Reformation in den nordischen Landern* (Munich, 1962) and, in collaboration with F. X. Seppelt, *Geschichte der Päpste, Von den Anfängen bis zur Gegenwart* (Munich, 1964).

MARIE-JOSEPH LE GUILLOU, O.P.: Born in France on December 25, 1920, he was ordained in 1947. He studied at the Sorbonne, the Saulchoir and the University of Athens. He gained doctorates in literature and theology in 1959, and after lecturing in Oriental theology and missiology at the Saulchoir he became director of ecumenical research at the Catholic Institute in Paris. His works include *Mission et Pauvreté, l'Heure de la Mission Mondiale* (Paris, 1964) and *Dialogue oecuménique* (Paris, 1962). He contributes to *Istina* and *Parole et Mission,* among others.

THOMAS McAVOY, C. S. C.: Born in the United States on September 12, 1903, he was ordained as a member of the Congregation of the Holy Cross in 1929. He studied at Notre Dame University, Holy Cross College, Washington, and Columbia University. He gained his M.A. and doctorate of philosophy in 1940, and since 1949 has been professor of history at

Notre Dame University. Among his publications are *The Great Crisis in American History, 1895–1900*. He is managing editor of *The Review of Politics*.

HEIKO OBERMAN: Born in Utrecht, the Netherlands, on October 15, 1930, he was ordained in the Presbyterian Church in 1958. He studied at the Universities of Utrecht and Oxford and received his doctorate in theology *cum laude* in 1957. He is professor of Church history at Tübingen, where he is also director of the Institute of Reformation History. He is a member of the American Academy of Arts and Sciences, of the American Society of Church History, and of the commission for the publication of Martin Luther's works. Among his published works are *The Harvest of Medieval Theology. Gabriel Biel and Late Medieval Nominalism* (Cambridge, U.S.A., 1963) and *Forerunners of the Reformation. The Shape of Late Medieval Thought* (New York, 1966).

BÉDA RIGAUX, O.F.M.: Born in Belgium on January 31, 1899, he was ordained in 1923. He studied at Louvain and gained his doctorate in theology. He was provincial of his order from 1945 to 1951, has been a professor of Scripture since 1924, and since 1956 has lectured at the Institute Supérieur des Sciences Religieuses, Louvain. His books include *L'Épître aux Thessaloniciens* (Collection Études Bibliques, 1956), *Témoignage de l'évangile de Marc* (1965) and *Témoignage de l'évangile de Matthieu* (1967). He is a member of the Biblical Commission and of the Commission of the Neo-Vulgate.

International Publishers of CONCILIUM

ENGLISH EDITION
Paulist Press
Glen Rock, N. J., U.S.A.

Burns & Oates Ltd.
25 Ashley Place
London, S.W.1

DUTCH EDITION
Uitgeverij Paul Brand, N. V.
Hilversum, Netherlands

FRENCH EDITION
Maison Mame
Tours/Paris, France

JAPANESE EDITION
Nansôsha
Tokyo, Japan

GERMAN EDITION
Verlagsanstalt Benziger & Co., A.G.
Einsiedeln, Switzerland

Matthias Grunewald-Verlag
Mainz, W. Germany

SPANISH EDITION
Ediciones Guadarrama
Madrid, Spain

PORTUGUESE EDITION
Livraria Morais Editora, Ltda.
Lisbon, Portugal

ITALIAN EDITION
Editrice Queriniana
Brescia, Italy